Mary Fitzgibbon

A Trip to Manitoba

Or, Roughing it on the Line

Mary Fitzgibbon

A Trip to Manitoba
Or, Roughing it on the Line

ISBN/EAN: 9783337141172

Printed in Europe, USA, Canada, Australia, Japan

Cover: Foto ©ninafisch / pixelio.de

More available books at **www.hansebooks.com**

A TRIP TO MANITOBA;

OR,

ROUGHING IT ON THE LINE.

BY

MARY FITZGIBBON.

Toronto:
ROSE-BELFORD PUBLISHING COMPANY.
MDCCCLXXX.

Entered according to Act of the Parliament of Canada, in the year one thousand eight hundred and eighty, by MARY FITZGIBBON, in the Office of the Minister of Agriculture.

DEDICATED

TO

Lady Dufferin.

PREFACE TO CANADIAN EDITION.

IT is one of the peculiarities of life in this "New World" that railways, which were first desired as a means of more readily carrying traffic already existing between towns, or entrepots of trade already built up, have come with us to be used as a means of settling the wilderness.

The backwoodsmen of forty years ago looked forward hopefully to the time when, his settlement having become populous and important enough, he might reasonably expect the extension of the railway system to his doors. The settler of to-day is unwilling to take up lands which are not within easy distance of at least a projected railway, if not one in course of construction.

The Canadian Pacific Railway, west of Winnipeg, is destined to be (as several Trunk lines south of it have been) a great colonization worker. Between Winnipeg and Lake Superior the line is a necessity to afford access from Canadian waters to the fertile lands of our great North-West. Its chances, as a colonization road, until those richer lands further on are filled up, are doubtless not very great. The country is, in a large part, rough and not easy to subdue by culture.

The plunge into this howling wilderness of wood, lake and rock, interspersed, and not rendered more valuable or romantic, by vast swamps or muskegs, to find a practicable railway route through it and build a line so far away from towns and the comforts of civilization, was a rough task for men. For women still harder, although it was but to accompany and care for them, to repeat in a new form what women have done when "roughing it in the bush" in the now settled parts of Canada forty years ago.

The writer of this sketch of rough life, under a novel combination of circumstances, with constant telegraphic communication with the outer world and railway work before them, has drawn a faithful picture, with a hope that it may be read with some interest now as a representation of one phase of the march of civilization into the wilderness and in the future, by those who go up to possess that goodly land, as a record of the rude work done to open a pathway for them to their new homes.

OTTAWA, *July, 1880.*

CONTENTS.

CHAPTER I.

                                                             PAGE

The Grand Trunk Railway—Sarnia—"Confusion worse confounded"—A Churlish Hostess—Fellow-Passengers on the *Manitoba*—"Off at last!"—Musical Honours—Sunrise on Lake Huron—A Scramble for Breakfast—An Impromptu Dance—The General Foe... 13

CHAPTER II.

Sault Ste. Marie—Indian Embroidery—Lake Superior—Preaching, Singing, and Card-playing—Silver Islet—Thunder Bay—The Dog River—Flowers at Fort William—"Forty Miles of Ice"—Icebergs and Warm Breezes—Duluth—Hotel Belles—Bump of Destructiveness in Porters..,..................... 23

CHAPTER III.

The Mississippi—The Rapids—Aerial Railway Bridges—Breakfast at Braynor—Lynch Law—Card-sharpers—Crowding in the Cars—Woman's Rights!—The Prairie—"A Sea of Fire"—Crookstown—Fisher's Landing—Strange Quarters—"The Express-Man's Bed"—Herding Like Sheep—On board the *Minnesota* 37

CHAPTER IV.

Red Lake River—Grand Forks—The Ferry—Custom-house Officers at Pembina—Mud and Misery—Winnipeg at last—A Walk through the Town—A Hospitable Welcome—Macadam wanted—Holy Trinity Church—A Picturesque Population—Indians shopping—An "All-sorts" Store—St. Boniface and its Bells—An Evening Scene 48

CHAPTER V.

Summer Days—The English Cathedral—Icelandic Emigrants—*Tableaux*—In chase of our Dinner—The Indian Summer—Blocked up—Gigantic Vegetables—Fruitfulness of the Country—Iceland Maidens—Rates of Wages—Society at Winnipeg—Half-breeds—Magic of the Red River Water—A Happy Hunting-ground—Where is Manitoba? 62

CHAPTER VI.

Winter Amusements—A Winnipeg Ball—Forty Degrees below Zero—New Year's Day—"Saskatchewan Taylor"—Indian Compliments—A Dog-train—Lost in the Snow—Amateur Theatricals—Sir Walter Raleigh's Hat—A Race with the Freshets—The Ice moves!—The First Steamer of the Season—Goodbye to Winnipeg.................................. 74

CHAPTER VII.

A Manitoban Travelling-carriage—The Perils of Short Cuts—The Slough of Despond—Paddy to the Rescue!—"Stick-in-the-Mud" and his Troubles—McQuade's—An Irish Welcome—Wretched Wanderers... 85

CHAPTER VIII.

Faithless Jehu—The "Blarney Stone"—Mennonites in search of News—"Water, Water everywhere"—A Herd of Buffaloes—A Mud Village—Pointe du Chêne and Old Nile—At Dawson Route—A Cheerful Party—*Toujours perdrix*—The "Best Room"—A Government Shanty—Cats and Dogs—Birch River—Mushroom-picking—The Mosquito Plague—A Corduroy Road—The Cariboo Muskeg.................... 97

CHAPTER IX.

PAGE

The "Nor'-west Angle"—The Company's House—Triumph of "Stick-in-the-Mud"—On the Lake of the Woods—A Gallant Cook—Buns à l'imprévu—A Man Overboard!—Camping out—Clear Water Bay—Our First Portage—A Noble Savage—How Lake Rice and Lake Deception won their Names—At our Journey's End 112

CHAPTER X.

Making a New Home—Carrière's Kitchen—The Navvies' Salle-à-Manger—A Curious Milking Custom—Insect Plagues—Peterboro' Canoes—Fishing Trips—Mail-day—Indian dread of drowning—The Indian Mail-carrier and his Partner—Talking by Telegraph—A Fire in the Woods............................. 125

CHAPTER XI.

Irish Wit—Bears ?—Death on the Red Pine Lake—A Grave in the Catholic Cemetery—The First Dog-train—A Christmas Fête—Compulsory Temperance—Contraband Goods—The Prisoner wins the Day—Whiskey on the Island—The Smuggler turned Detective—A Fatal Frolic—"Mr. K——'s Legs" 137

CHAPTER XII.

Birds of Passage—An Independent Swede—By Sleigh to Ostersund—A Son of the Forest—Burnt out—A Brave Canadian Girl—Roughing it in the Shanty—The Kitchen-tent—Blasting the Rock—The Perils of Nitro-glycerine—Bitter Jests.................. 151

CHAPTER XIII.

We lose our Cows—Cahill promoted—Gardening on a New Principle — Onions in Hot-houses—Cahill is hoaxed—Martin the Builder — How the Navvies lived—Sunday in Camp—The Cook's Leap—That "Beautiful Skunk!"—Wild Fruits—Parting...... 165

CHAPTER XIV.

For Ostersund—Lake Lulu—Giant Rocks and Pigmy Mortals—The Island Garden—Heaven's Artillery—Strange Casualty at the Ravine—My Luggage nearly blown up—The Driver's Presence of Mind—How to carry a Canoe—Darlington Bay—An Invisible Lake—Lord and Lady Dufferin—A Paddle to the Rapids—The Captain's Tug—Monopoly of Water-carriage—Indian Legends—The Abode of Snakes......... 177

CHAPTER XV.

Clear Water Bay transformed—Cahill's Farewell—Ptarmigan Bay—A Night under Canvas—"No more Collars or Neckties!"—Companions in Misfortune—Cedar Lake—"Lop-sticks"—An Indian Village—Shashegheesh's Two Wives—Buying Potatoes—*Seniores Priores*—Excellent Carrots!—Frank's Flirtations with the Squaws—The Dogs eat Carrière's Toboggan 192

CHAPTER XVI.

Falcon River—An Unlucky Supper—The Fate of our Fried Pork—A Weary Paddle—A Sundial in the wilderness—A Gipsy Picnic—"Floating away"—The Dried Musk-rats—Falcon Lake—How can we land?—Mr. M—— "in again"—Surprised by Indians—How we dried our Clothes—The Last Night in Camp 206

CHAPTER XVII.

Indian Loyalty—A Nap on Falcon Lake—A False Alarm—The Power of Whisky—"Magnificent Water Stretches"—A Striking Contrast—Picnic Lake—How we crossed Hawk Lake—Long Pine Lake—Bachelors' Quarters at Ingolf—We dress for Dinner

—Our Last Portage—A Rash Choice—" Grasp your Nettle "— Mr. F——'s Gallantry—Cross Lake — Denmark's Ranche—A Tramp through the Mire.. 218

CHAPTER XVIII.

Tilford—Pedestrians under Difficulties—The Railway at last—Not exactly a First-class Carriage—The Jules Muskeg—Whitemouth and Broken-Head Rivers— Vagaries of the Engine-driver—The Hotel at St. Boniface—Red River Ferry—Winnipeg—"A Vagabond Heroine"—The Terrier at fault............. 235

CHAPTER XIX.

The *Minnesota* again—Souvenirs of Lord and Lady Dufferin—From Winnipeg by Red River—*Compagnons de Voyage*—A Model Farm—" Bees "—Manitoba a good Field for Emigrants — Changes at Fisher's Landing—A Mild Excitement for Sundays—Racing with Prairie Fires—Glyndon—Humours of a Pullman Sleeping Car—Lichfield 247

CHAPTER XX.

Lakes Smith and Howard—Lovely Lake Scenery—Long Lake—The Little American—" Wait till you see our Minnetaunka!"—Minneanopolis—Villa Hotels—A

PAGE

Holiday Town—The Great Flour Mills—St. Paul's—Our American Cousins—The French Canadian's Story — Kind-hearted Fellow-passengers — A New Way of Travelling together—The Mississippi—Milwaukee, the Prettiest Town in Wisconsin — School-houses—A Peep at Chicago—Market Prices—Pigs !—The Fairy Tales of Progress—Scotch Incredulity—Detroit Ferry—Hamilton—Good-by to my Readers. 258

A
TRIP TO MANITOBA.

CHAPTER I.

The Grand Trunk Railway—Sarnia—"Confusion worse confounded"—A Churlish Hostess—Fellow-Passengers on the *Manitoba*—"Off at last!"—Musical Honours—Sunrise on Lake Huron—A Scramble for Breakfast—An Impromptu Dance—The General Foe.

AFTER a long day's journey on the Grand Trunk Railway, without even the eccentricities of fellow-passengers in our Pullman car to amuse us, we were all glad to reach Sarnia. The monotony of the scenery through which we passed had been unbroken, except by a prettily situated cemetery, and the tasteful architecture of a hillside church, surrounded by trees just putting on their spring foliage.

It was eight o'clock when we reached the wharf, and the steamer *Manitoba* only waited for our arrival to cast loose her moorings and enter the dark blue waters of Lake Huron. "Haste" will not express the excitement of the scene. Men, rushing hither and thither in search of friends, traps, and luggage, were goaded to fury by the calmness of the officials and their determination not to be hurried. Hearing there was no chance of having tea on board that night, and discovering near the wharf a signboard announcing that meals could be obtained at all hours (except, as we were told, that particular one), we with difficulty persuaded the proprietress to let us have something to eat. Amidst muttered grumblings that she was "slaved to death," that her "life was not worth a rap," and so on, every remark being emphasized with a plate or dish, we were at last supplied with bread, cheese, and beefsteak, for which we were kindly allowed to pay fifty cents each.

The scene on board the boat beggars description. The other steamers being still ice-bound on Lake Superior, the *Manitoba* was obliged to take as much freight and as many passengers as she could carry, many of the latter having been waiting in Sarnia upwards of ten days for her departure. Surveying parties, immigrants of almost every nation on their way to make homes in the great North-West, crowded the decks and gangways. The confusion of tongues, the shrill cries of the frightened and tired children, the oaths of excited men, and the trundling and thumping of the baggage, mingled with the shrieks of adjacent engines "made night hideous." Porters and cabmen jostled women laden with baskets of linen, brought on board at the last minute, when the poor tired stewardess had no time to administer the well-merited reprimand; passengers rushed about in search of the purser, anxious to secure their state-rooms before they were usurped by some one else.

It was midnight when the commotion had subsided, and quarters were assigned to all but a stray man or two wandering about in search of some Mr. Brown or Mr. Jones, whose room he was to share. Climbing into my berth, I soon fell asleep; but only for a few moments. The shrill whistle, the vehement ringing of the captain's bell, the heavy beat of the paddles, roused me; and as we left the wharf and steamed out from among the ships and small craft dotting the water on every side, " Off at last ! " was shouted from the crowded decks. Then the opening bars of " God save the Queen " were sung heartily and not inharmoniously, followed by three cheers for her Majesty, three for her Imperial Highness, three for her popular representative Lord Dufferin, and so on, till the enthusiasm culminated in " He's a jolly good fellow ; " the monotony of which sent me to sleep again.

At four o'clock next morning I scrambled out of my berth at the imminent risk of broken bones, wondering why the inventive powers of our Yankee neighbours had not hit upon some arrangement to facilitate the descent; dressed, and went in search of fresh air. Picking my steps quietly between sleeping forms—for men in almost every attitude, some with blankets or great-coats rolled round them, were lying on the floor and lounges in the saloon— I reached the deck just as the sun rose above the broad blue waters, brightening every moment the band of gold where sky and water met. Clouds of ink-black smoke floated from our funnel, tinged by the rising sun with every shade of yellow, red, and brown. Mirrored in the calm water below, lay the silent steamer—silent, save for the ceaseless revolution of her paddles, whose monotonous throb seemed like the beating of a great heart.

For an hour or more I revelled in the beauty of water and sky, and ceased to wonder why people born on the coast love the sea so dearly, and pine for the sight of its waves. When the men came to wash the decks, a pleasant brawny fellow told me we were likely to have a good run up the lakes. The storms of the last few days having broken up the ice, and driven it into the open, there was hope both of the ice-locked steamers getting out, and of our getting into Duluth without much trouble—" unless the wind changes, which is more than possible," he added abruptly; and walked off, as if fearful of my believing his sanguine predictions too implicitly.

Later the passengers appeared, grumbling at the cold, and at being obliged to turn out so early, and wishing breakfast were ready. Of this wished-for meal the clatter of dishes in the saloon soon gave welcome warning. Dickens says that when, before taking his first meal on board an American steamer, " he tore after the rushing crowd to see what was wrong, dreadful visions of fire, in its most aggravated form, floated through his mind ; but it was only *dinner* that the hungry public were rushing to devour." We were nearly as bad on the *Manitoba*, the friendly steward warning most of us to secure our seats without delay, the cabin-walls being gradually lined with people on either side, each behind a chair. One of the "boys" strode ostentatiously down the long saloon, ringing a great hand-bell, which summoned a mixed multitude pell-mell to the scene of action, only to retreat in disappointment at finding the field already occupied.

It was amusing to watch the different expressions on the faces down the lines while waiting for breakfast. Men, chiefly surveyors, who during their annual trips to and from work had got used to " that sort of thing," took it coolly ; judiciously choosing a seat directly opposite their state-room door, or standing in the background, but near enough to expel any intruder. New men, looking as uncomfortable as if they had been caught in petty larceny, twisted their youthful moustaches, put their hands in their pockets, or leant against the wall, trying to look perfectly indifferent as to the event; some of their neighbours smiling satirically at their folly. Old farmer-looking bodies, grumbling at the crush, mingled with Yankees, toothpick in hand, ready for business; sturdy Englishmen whom one knew appreciated creature comforts; and dapper little Frenchmen, hungry yet polite. Here stood a bright-looking Irishwoman, who vainly tried to restrain the impatience of five or six children, whose faces still shone from the friction of their morning ablutions; there, an old woman well-nigh double with age, who, rather than be separated from the two stalwart sons by her side, was going to end her days in a strange land. Here was a group of bright, chatty little French Canadians, with the usual superabundance of earrings and gay ribbons decorating their persons; there a great raw-boned Scotchwoman, inwardly lamenting the porridge of her native land, frowned upon the company.

The bell ceased, and—" Presto!" all were seated,

and turning over their plates as if for a wager. Then came a confused jumble of tongues, all talking at once; the rattle of dishes, the clatter of knives and forks, and the rushing about of the boy-waiters. It required quick wit to choose a breakfast dish, from the "White-fish-finanhaddie-beefsteak-cold roast beef-muttonchop-bacon-potatoes-toast-roll-brown bread-or-white-tea-or-coffee," shouted breathlessly by a youth on one side, while his comrade screamed the same, in a shrill falsetto, to one's neighbour on the other; their not starting simultaneously making the confusion worse confounded. Such was the economical mode of setting forth the bill of fare on the *Manitoba*. There were three hundred and fifty people on board; more than one-third of whom were cabin, or would-be cabin, passengers. The accommodation being insufficient, some were camping on the upper deck, some in the saloon, many on the stairs, and others wherever elbow-room could be found. Breakfast began at half-past seven, and at half-past nine the late risers were still at it; and it was not long before the same thing (only more so!), in the shape of dinner, had to be gone through.

As Lake Huron was calm and our boat steady, we had more " God save the Queen " after dinner, besides " Rule Britannia " and other patriotic songs, several of the passengers playing the piano very well. Some one also played a violin, and the men, clearing the saloon of sofas, and superfluous chairs, danced a double set of quadrilles, after having tried in vain to persuade some of the emigrant girls to become their partners. They were an amusing group—from the grinning steward, who, cap on head, figured away through all the steps he could recollect or invent (some of them marvels of skill and agility in their way), to the solemn young man, only anxious to do his duty creditably. But alas for the short-lived joviality of the multitude! After touching at Southampton the boat altered her course, and the effect of her occasional rolls in the trough of the waves soon became manifest.

One by one the less courageous of the crowd crept away. Every face soon blanched with terror at the common enemy. Wretched women feebly tried to help crying children, though too ill to move themselves; others threw them down anywhere, to be able to escape in time for the threatened paroxysm; all were groaning, wan and miserable, railing at the poor, wearied stewardess, calling her here, there, and everywhere at the same time, and threatening her as if she were the sole cause of their woe. About midnight, our course being altered, "Richard was himself again."

CHAPTER II.

Sault Ste. Marie—Indian Embroidery—Lake Superior—Preaching, Singing, and Card-playing—Silver Islet—Thunder Bay—The Dog River—Flowers at Fort William—" Forty Miles of Ice "—Icebergs and Warm Breezes—Duluth—Hotel Belles—Bump of Destructiveness in Porters.

THE scenery just before entering the St. Mary River, which unites Lake Huron and Lake Superior, is very fine. As the steamer threaded the group of islands with their high, rocky, picturesquely wooded shores, we were sometimes near enough to distinguish the many varieties of mosses and ferns just springing into life; then, steaming across the rippling water, we reached some point whose distant beauty had made us long to carry away more than a memory of its outlines; and so, winding in and out amongst the islands of this North American archipelago, we "fetched" the Sault Ste. Marie about sunset.* The "Sault," as it is generally called, is a pretty little village, situated at the foot of a hill on the north shore of the canal. Having to remain an hour there, we went ashore, up the long straight street, to a frame-house, or store, where there was an extensive display of Indian work. The Lake Superior and Huron Indians are particularly noted

---

* The island-studded northern expanse of Lake Huron is known as Georgian Bay. As the level of Lake Superior is between thirty and forty feet higher than that of Lake Huron, there is a corresponding fall at the head of the St. Mary River. This difference of level prevents direct navigation between the two lakes; consequently, the Americans have constructed across the extreme north-eastern point of the State of Michigan a fine canal, which gives them exclusive possession of the entrance by water to the great inland sea of Lake Superior. When, in 1870, the Red River Expedition, under Colonel (now General Sir) Garnet Wolseley, sought to make the passage in several steamboats *en route* for Thunder Bay, the State authorities of Michigan issued a prohibition against it. Fortunately, the Cabinet of Washington overruled this prohibition, and the Expedition was permitted to pass; not, however, until valuable time had been lost. Considering the importance of this canal to the Dominion Government, and that at a crisis the United States' Cabinet could close Lake Superior to our vessels of war, I think some steps should be taken by which the Imperial Government would become joint proprietors of the canal, with an equal share in its management at all times.

for the beauty of their embroidery on skins, silk, birch bark, and cloth, in beads, porcupine quills, or silk. Their imitative genius is so great that the squaws can copy anything, and I know people who have had their crests and coats-of-arms embroidered upon their tobacco-pouches and belts, from an impression on paper or sealing-wax. Generally they copy flowers and ferns, invent their own patterns, or, what seems even more wonderful, make them by chewing a piece of bark into the form they require —the bark assuming the appearance of a stamped braiding pattern. As the white people put an exorbitant price on the flour and trinkets they give in exchange for the Indian's work, the latter ask, when selling for money, what seems more than its full value; but many who travel that way provided with cheap trinkets and gaudy ribbons, get the work cheaply enough.

There is quite a large Roman Catholic church in the village; but we had to be content with a tiptoe peep through its windows, as after the "angelus" the door is locked. There are some small trading stores, a few scattered houses, long, pretty winding roads up the hills, skirted by cozy little farmhouses and wheat fields, and one or two more dwellings of more pretension occupied as summer residences by Americans. A little higher up, on the other side of the canal, lie the low white buildings of the American fort. That fortification, with its sentries and the national flag floating over the chief bastion, looked gay enough in the rays of the fast-setting sun. After remaining several hours to coal, we left the little village in the darkness, and when day dawned again found ourselves out in the broad waters of Lake Superior—called by the Indians "the Great Sea" (*Kitchee Kumma*). For hours no land was to be seen on either side, but we were visited by two little birds, quivering with cold, weary from their long flight, almost too timid to alight upon our boat, yet too tired to resist the resting-place. Poor little wanderers! many a lonely emigrant, who had left all he loved behind to try his fortune in an unknown land, felt sympathy for them.

Seeing nothing but water and sky to interest us without, we turned our attention to our fellow-passengers within. At one end of the long saloon a zealous Cecilite, the centre of a mixed group, was "improving the occasion," Bible in hand—exhorting his hearers to turn from the error of their ways, and denouncing the world and its wickedness, as exemplified in the group of card-players close by. Their "I'll order it up!" "Pass!" "I'll play it alone!" mingled with the grave accents of the preacher, whose exhortations were answered by shouts of laughter and ringing glees from the other end of the boat, where stood the piano and its satellites. In vain the poor Cecilite tried "to stem the torrent" of what he considered " Satan's doings;" his obstinacy and want of tact only increased the mischievous delight of his enemies. At the sides of the saloon small knots of French Canadians chatted merrily; at the top of the stairs an emigrant or two were allowed to infringe the rule of " no deck passengers," because of the crowd on board. Poor things! One did not wonder that they escaped gladly from the jarring sounds and offensive smells below.

Early on Saturday morning we passed Silver Islet, that mine of wealth to our neighbours across the line. It lies in an island-dotted bay, and is so covered with mining works that it looks like a pile of buildings rising out of the water. The crushing-mills are on the mainland close by. Silver Islet first belonged to a Canadian company; but from the lack of enterprise or capital it was sold to an American company for a nominal sum, and, as is often the case, the sanguine nature of Cousin Jonathan, acting on the motto, "Nothing venture nothing win," has been successful, and the company is now (1879) shipping $20,000 worth of silver ore a day. The islet can be visited only by those who have especial permission to see the mines and works, or friends among the officials, neither of which had we.

The adjacent village, at which the *Manitoba* stopped, did not look as if times were very prosperous with it. Two smoky little tugs lay idly at the small wharf, and the few red wooden houses built against the rocks, their flat roofs piled up with the bales of goods and boxes—the ever-present blue barrels of coal-oil being most conspicuous—seemed tenantless. Leaving Silver Islet far behind, we rounded Whitefish Point, with its tall lighthouse, and saw a very distinct mirage—a long stretch of cold blue water, filled with great blocks of ice. It was rather amusing to see the eagerness with which glasses were levelled at the " counterfeit presentment" of a scene, of whose reality we should soon have even too much.

At the entrance of Thunder Bay, we passed Thunder Cape on our right and Pie Island on our left; the former, a bold promontory, rising 1300 feet above the sea-level, and wooded with a short stunted growth of bush, principally poplar. Save for its picturesquely situated lighthouse and log hut, where the keeper lives, no other sign of habitation was visible. Thunder Bay and Cape probably take their names from the fierce and frequent storms that rage there; Pie Island from the peculiar formation of its northern end. Passing many rocky islands, with tiny waterfalls zigzaging down their sides, we arrived at "Prince Arthur's Landing" and walked up the long pier, partly roofed to form a temporary warehouse for a pile of freight, in the teeth of a blistering hot land-breeze, which drove the dust in blinding, choking eddies about us. After looking at some specimens of Lake Superior agate, which were on exhibition in a dusty shop, and buying some

c

lemons at what we thought the exorbitant price of a dollar and a half per dozen, we were glad to retrace our steps to the steamer, where we found the captain ready and anxious to start.

Half an hour's steaming brought us to the mouth of the Kaministiquia, or Dog River, and entering it, we were at once in another country. No more dusty roads, baked-looking piers, nor begrimed aborigines; but bright rippling water, cool green fields, dotted here and there with leafy trees, cattle grazing or lying lazily in their shade, trim fences, long grass-grown country roads, and soon the white walls and flowery garden of Fort William, the Hudson Bay Company's trading post. The rockery in the centre of the garden would have gladdened the heart of an Ontario gardener. I believe that wealthy people there have had large fragments of Lake Superior rock brought down to adorn their lawns and gardens. We found friends at the fort in the factor and his family, with whom we spent a pleasant half-hour. Mr. McIntyre is well known, and many will owe him gratitude for his kindness as long as Fort William or the Canada Pacific Railway remains in their memory.

We left Thunder Bay for Duluth at three o'clock. The day had become cloudy, and showers fell all the evening, but not heavily enough to prevent every man, woman, and child from rushing out to " speak " the down-coming boat *Ontario*, and hear her report on the state of the ice-fields. She had been six days ice-bound at Duluth, and the answer to our captain's inquiry was—

"Forty miles of ice; only one passage. If you hit that, all right; if not, you won't get through."

And wishing us luck and good night, with three hearty cheers from either deck, we parted. Naturally anxious as we were for a speedy journey, the possibility of failure in hitting the one open passage lent the additional charm of uncertainty to our voyage; not charming, however, to the poor emigrants whose stock of provisions was too scanty to admit of a long stay on board, while the commissariat of the steamer was not prepared to supply them. Knowing this, the captain—a pleasant, handsome man—quoting the saying that " Fortune favours the brave," put on steam.

By eight o'clock on Sunday morning we had met

great blocks of ice, and grown accustomed to hearing them bump against the side of the boat; and before noon we were well into the ice-fields, with loose blocks of ice on every side, and a rough surface of piled-up masses as far as the eye could see. Up a narrow strip of blue water we steamed, the passage closing in our wake. Then the way became blocked ahead, while the vessel heeled to one side with a lurch, as a great block went under her keel. The captain held on steadily but slowly, stopping the machinery until a large berg was passed, and taking advantage of an opening created by the waves as they bore the floes upon their crests. As the ice-blocks closed in behind us the certainty of being unable to return, and the difficulty of going ahead, gave increased excitement to our adventure.

One of its strangest features was the heat. Though clothed in the lightest summer dresses, we were uncomfortably warm—and this with miles of ice around us! The warm land-breeze, and our captain's promptitude and determination, enabled us to reach Duluth that evening. A change of wind the same night drove the ice back into the bay, and from the hotel windows we saw and commiserated four vessels locked fast, their crews and passengers suffering from cold and short rations for four days. The change of wind made us glad of our fur jackets.

Duluth, situated on the rocky north, or Minnesota, shore of the extreme western end of Lake Superior —otherwise St. Louis Bay—was apparently planned in expectation of its one day becoming the principal centre of commerce between America and Canada— in short the great capital of the lakes. Everything is on a large scale. The streets are broad; the wharves and warehouses extensive; the hotels immense; the custom house and other public buildings massive and capacious enough to accommodate any number of extra clerks when the rush of business shall come—a rush which is still in the future. During the day and a half we spent there, the hotel omnibus and one other team were the only locomotives, and a lame man and a water-carrier with a patch over his eye the only dwellers in Duluth we saw; while the people from our boat seemed to be the only visitors who woke the echoes in the sleepy place. It was like a city in a fairy tale, over which a spell had been cast; its very cleanliness was depressing, and so suggestive of disuse, that I think a mass of mud scraped off the road might have given some appearance of traffic and life to the scene.

There *are* people in Duluth, however, though it is difficult to say where they hide themselves; for some of our party went to service in a little church on a hill, and came back charmed with the eloquence of the clergyman and the sweetness of the voices in the quartette choir, to say nothing of several pretty girls they noticed amongst the congregation. Still, Duluth will always seem to me like a city in a dream. On the opposite, or Wisconsin shore of the lake, is Superior City, a pretty, half-built town, rising slowly into commercial importance. Unfortunately we were unable to cross to it.

I cannot leave Deluth without speaking of the "girls" in the hotel, as they were called, in order not to wound the sensitive democracy of the Yankee nature, which abhors the name of servant. There were three in the great dining-saloon, whose superabundance of empty chairs and tables gave even greater dreariness to the house than its long, empty corridors. Pretty fair girls they were, neat in dress, but so tightly laced that it was painful to look at them. Their slow, stiff, automatic movements were suggestive of machinery, and in keeping with the sleepy spell cast over the town. All the lithe, living gracefulness of their figures was destroyed for the sake of drawing in an inch or two of belt. Watching them, I attacked my breakfast with greater energy, to prove to myself that there was something substantial about the premises.

One word respecting the treatment of luggage in that part of the world by porters and officials, whose organ of destructiveness seems to be abnormally developed. Boxes are thrown pell-mell into the hold, or tossed on end out of high baggage-vans, with such unnecessary violence that nothing less than cases of solid iron or stronger metal could have stood it. Trunks, "stationary" boxes warranted to stand any ill-usage, were cracked and broken; and the poor emigrants' boxes, of comparatively slight construction, soon became a mass of ruins, with their contents scattered on the ground. It was the same everywhere—at Duluth, at Glyndon, and at Fisher's Landing, where we took the Red River boat. At Glyndon half the baggage was piled on an open truck, and the heavy rain we passed through that night completed the ruin the officials began. A member of the Hudson Bay Company, who had travelled a great deal over this continent, said he found it best to carry his baggage in a small hand-valise, or in a very large trunk so heavy that it required two men to move it; anything between the two was invariably smashed.

CHAPTER III.

The Mississippi—The Rapids—Aerial Railway Bridges—
Breakfast at Braynor—Lynch Law—Card-sharpers—
Crowding in the Cars—Woman's Rights!—The Prairie—
"A Sea of Fire"—Crookstown—Fisher's Landing—
Strange Quarters—"The Express-Man's Bed"—Herding
Like Sheep—On board the *Minnesota*.

AFTER leaving Duluth at four o'clock on Tuesday morning by rail, the country through which we passed was very beautiful. Lake succeeded lake, then came wooded hills and tiny mountain streams, crossed by high bridges. These bridges were without parapets, and so narrow that, looking out of the window of the car, one saw a deep gorge sixty or seventy feet below. One railway bridge across the Mississippi—a narrow enough stream there, at least to eyes accustomed to the broad St. Lawrence—was more than seventy feet high, and so unsafe that trains were allowed only to creep slowly across it. The rapids on the St. Louis River, along the banks of which the Northern Pacific runs, are magnificent. For some miles the high banks occasionally almost shut out the view; then, as the train winds round a sharp curve, a mountain torrent of foaming water bursts upon the gaze. Rocks tower above it, with great trees bending from their heights; in the stream are huge boulders round which the water whirls and hisses, sending its spray high over the rugged banks, in every nook and crevice of which grow long ferns and graceful wild-flowers. Then follows a long smooth stretch of water with grassy wooded shores, and through the trees one catches distant glimpses of yet wider and more beautiful falls than those just passed.

We breakfasted at Braynor at nine o'clock, and heard with pleasure that we had forty-five minutes wherein to satisfy exhausted nature. Everything was delicious, and we should have done the fare even greater justice had we known that it was the last good meal we should obtain for thirty-six hours. When we returned to the car we were greatly amused by an irrepressible fellow-traveller, whose over-politeness and loquacity savoured of a morning dram or two. He insisted on pointing out the exact spot —marked by a tall, rough-looking post with a cross-tree on it, that stood near the rails—where two Indians had been "lynched" for some crime by the citizens; which exploit being regarded with *pardonable* pride by them, was boasted of to travellers accordingly. Volumes might be written on Yankee oppression of the poor Red-skins, and yet leave the disgraceful story but half told.

Our train was crowded, and during the morning two rather well-dressed black-eyed men came on board. The conductor told us they were the pests of that part of the road—three card-monté men—and that, in spite of being carefully warned, many travellers, especially amongst the well-to-do-farmer class emigrating to Manitoba, were daily fleeced by them, there being no apparent redress, as they are sharp enough to evade any direct breach of the law. These men succeeded in drawing two boys of eighteen or twenty into their toils, and obtained possession of their watches, as well as all the money they had about them. When the lads protested vehemently, the sharpers offered to return the former upon receipt of five dollars, which they knew their victims did not possess. To our great relief, the men got off at the station where we stopped for dinner.

We changed trains at Glyndon for the branch line, then only recently laid to Fisher's Landing, but since that time continued to the frontier station of Pembina. There was only one passenger car to hold all those who had comfortably filled three on the other line, and it would be difficult to convey any idea of the crowding and crushing that ensued to obtain seats, and pack away the numerous travelling-bags, and provision-baskets brought by the emigrants from Ontario. Having gentlemen with us, we were soon provided for; but just before the train started a very dirty, fashionably dressed young woman, carrying an equally dirty baby, came in. Looking about her, and not finding a vacant seat, she said in an insolent tone, giving her head a toss:—

"No seats? Wall, I guess I ain't agoin' to stand and hold this here heavy child!" and sat down in my lap. I had, like most people, often been "sat upon," figuratively, during my life, but never literally, and it was with some difficulty that I managed to extricate myself. The girl next proceeded, with the assistance of a dirty pocket-handkerchief and the tin drinking-mug belonging to the car, to perform her toilet and that of her infant; her efforts resulting in a streakiness of dirt on both faces, where the colour had been uniform before.

We were on the prairie—the great rolling prairie, at last; and I was disappointed—nothing but grass and sky, desolate and lonely. These, however, were my first impressions. How fond I grew of the prairie I know now that I am away from it; perhaps for ever. Towards night, black clouds gathered in the sky, and distant thunder heralded the coming of one of those great storms for which the prairie is so famous. The air was so charged with electricity that the train had to be stopped several times, and the wheels of the cars drenched with water to prevent their taking fire. As night closed in, incessant flashes of white sheet lightning almost blinded us. Each white flash was riven by red forks of flame, until with the horizon one constant blaze, the plain seemed a vast sea of fire. Over our heads, in great zigzag lines, shot the fire fluid, as the thunder rattled, roared, crashed, and broke around us; then, in a momentary lull, came torrents of rain, rushing madly across the sward, and drowning the noise of the fast flying-train, as if some fiend upon a diabolical errand were borne through the warring elements. It seemed as though two or three storms had met, to contend for mastery; flashes of white, yellow, and red lightning outdid each other in brilliancy, and peals of thunder, near and distant, reverberated in quick succession. No one who has encountered a rain-storm on the prairie can form an idea of its grandeur and force.

During a short lull in the storm, we stopped at a place called Crookstown for tea, following a touter of the "*Ho*-tel" there—or rather a railway lantern, as the darkness completely hid the man—through mud and water up to our ankles; over stumps and sticks; through a dilapidated gateway, stoup, and wash-house, to a long, low room, where the table was laid for tea. Seated round it on benches, chairs, three-legged stools —in fact, on anything they could get hold of—were the engine-driver, conductor, express-man, and other officials. The meal consisted of bread and butter, potatoes boiled in their jackets, fried bacon swimming in fat, and scalding tea in handleless cups. Asking for eggs, we were told that there was not one to be had in the "town." Query, what is a town? Crookstown could not boast of half a dozen houses besides the station.

Another hour's journey brought us to Fisher's Landing, on Red Lake River, where we were to remain until next morning. Although the boat was at the landing, we were not allowed to go on board until all the freight was shipped. This intelligence was given us by a rakish-looking Yankee, who added that his "Hotel" was the best in the place, and if we would come "right along" he would give us rooms for the night. Gathering up our traps, and thinking we could not do much worse than remain in the crowded car all night, we followed, paddling through the mud to the much-boasted "Ho-tel." This was a house built of boards, the entrance room or office having a high desk or counter across one corner; a recess under the stairs in the other containing a bench, on which were ranged two or three pails and a basin, while on the wall hung the general towel, looking rather the worse for wear. A room opening from the recess had a table set like the one at Crookstown, apparently for breakfast; the floors were literally covered with mud. What, we surmised, can the bedrooms be like in such a place? Our question was only too soon answered. Presently a shaggy-headed, untidy woman made her appearance, hastily fastening her clothes. She was very cross, and grumbled that there were only two rooms, but that she would take one of us in with her (an offer which was politely declined), and snappishly ordered a man to show the way upstairs. Clambering up a steep flight of steps after our conductor and his lantern, we were ushered into a room containing a bed—which had all the appearance of having been slept in for a week—a rocking chair, and a bureau; a smaller room opening out of it also contained a very-much-slept-in bed. Throwing open the door of the latter room with a flourish that would have been creditable in a professional showman, he introduced us.

"This, ladies, you can have. Two can sleep here nicely. True, the bed has not been made, but I can soon settle that!" and putting his lantern on the floor, he gave the bed a poke or two, and tried to smooth the frowsy-looking coverlet.

"Oh, that's the express-man's bed!" he said, in answer to our inquiry as to who was to occupy the outer room. "Must have it, you know; always stops here. The best room in the town!"

Seeing that we did not appear satisfied, he added—

"You can lock your door" (there was a whole board a foot wide out of the partition); "and, after all, it's only the express-man; you needn't mind him. Then in the morning you can sit here, for he is off early, and we make it the ladies' sitting-room." And drawing the rocking-chair to the window, he set it going.

But as we still *did* object to the express-man's proximity, he led the way to another room, about the same size, but with a door that we could latch, a bunk bed, a wooden box, and for toilet apparatus, a yellow pudding-bowl, and white jug full of water. With some difficulty we succeeded in getting a lamp, and spreading our rugs over the bed, we lay down. When the tramping about downstairs ceased, sometime after midnight, we dozed until morning. I was up first, and, going downstairs in search of water, could not help laughing at the absurd sight of a row of legs and dangling braces under the stairway, the heads belonging to them being bent over the pails I had noticed there the night before. Seven men had slept on the floor of the express-man's room that night, for which accommodation they paid three dollars. During the day some twenty women emigrants, who were obliged to leave the car, taking refuge there from the mud and rain, were charged twenty-five cents a head; and, as a concession, children were taken at half-price.

Breakfast was a repetition of the supper at Crookstown, and although blessed with excellent appetites generally, we lost them completely at Fisher's Landing. About noon, we smuggled ourselves on board the *Minnesota*, and a few judicious tips enabled us to take up our quarters there at once. How we did enjoy our dinner! Never did fish, flesh, or fowl taste so good, and we felt compelled to apologize to the steward for the emptiness of the dishes he carried away. However, he did not appear astonished, as the bill of fare at the "*Ho*-tel" was well known.

It was Thursday morning before all the freight was stowed away and we could leave the landing—or "Fisher's," as *habitués* of the road call it. The *Minnesota* is a very comfortable boat, and with the exception of one or two farmers and their families, and an old Frenchwoman, we had her to ourselves. The captain was a genial, large-hearted Yankee, the steward and pretty little maid were very attentive; and, by contrast with the "*Ho*-tel," we thought ourselves in pleasant quarters.

CHAPTER IV.

Red Lake River—Grand Forks—The Ferry—Custom-house Officers at Pembina—Mud and Misery—Winnipeg at last—A Walk through the Town—A Hospitable Welcome—Macadam wanted—Holy Trinity Church—A Picturesque Population—Indians shopping—An "All-sorts" Store—St. Boniface and its Bells—An Evening Scene.

RED Lake River flows into Red River at Grand Forks, some twelve or thirteen miles below Fisher's Landing. It is much the narrower stream, with so many bends that when we were not running headlong into the left bank we grounded on the right. The boat frequently formed a bridge from one bend to the other, and heads were ducked down or drawn back suddenly to avoid having eyes scratched out by the spreading boughs of beech and hazel which stretched over the stream. It was nothing unusual to find our course impeded by a large branch becoming so entangled in the wheel at the stern, that men had to get down and chop it away before the boat could proceed.

At Grand Forks, where there is a Hudson Bay Company's trading post, a billiard saloon, hotel, general store, and post-office all in one, and a few smaller houses, the ferry is a large flat-bottomed sort of platform, railed on either side and fastened to a long thick rope stretched across the river. When there is a load to ferry over, this platform is let loose from the shore, and the current carries it across, the rope keeping it from going down stream. The shores of Red River are almost bare; a few miserable poplars here and there, one or two small log-houses and mud-built huts from which wild, dirty Indians emerged to watch the boat pass, were all we saw upon them. The banks are for the most part so high that only from the upper deck could we see inland.

The frontier post, Pembina, is well known as the spot beyond which in 1869 the rebel Louis Riel, the "Little Napoleon" of Red River, would not allow Mr. McDougall, the "lieutenant-governor of Manitoba," appointed by the Canadian administration, to pass. Here we had a visit from the custom-house officers. They were good specimens of their different countries. The Canadian was a round, fat, jolly, handsome, fair man; the Yankee was tall, slight, and black-eyed, with a cadaverous look, increased by his close-fitting mackintosh and cowl. They did not give us any trouble, and I felt sorry for their lonely life, and the pounds of mud they had to carry with them everywhere.

Such mud! There is no wharf or planking of any kind, and all freight and baggage is landed on (or into) the muddy bank. Barrels rolled through it became unrecognizable, and were doubled in weight before they reached their warehouse. Men worked on bare feet, with trousers rolled to their knees, and the slippery swashy look of everything was horrible. An Indian (not of the Fenimore Cooper type) leant against an old cooking-stove stranded on the bank, and an old squaw squatted on a heap of dirty straw watching with lack lustre eyes the disembarkation. A mile or two above Pembina is the American fort, with its trim barracks, fortifications, mounted guns, sentries, and some military life about it. Near it is the house built by Captain Cameron, R.E., when in charge of the International Boundary Survey. The remainder of our journey up the Red River of the North was uninteresting, and we hailed with delight our arrival at Winnipeg, on Saturday morning, the 4th of June.

It took some time to disembark from the *Minnesota*. The emigrants had been up at daylight, and after making haste to get their property together, found that they had to wait the arrival of the custom-house officer. At about eight o'clock, a waggon being procured to take our luggage, we, carrying our travelling-bags and shawls, walked—for there were no cabs nor omnibuses—into Winnipeg.

The *Minnesota* had stopped at the old custom-house wharf, the bulk of her freight being for that end of the town, and we had to traverse the entire length of Winnipeg to reach Mrs. T——, who had kindly invited us to remain with her until Mrs. C—— could find a suitable house. Up narrow, rickety planks, through mud and mire, past two log-houses fast falling into ruin—which were pointed out as having been the only houses in Winnipeg, besides the Fort Garry settlement, ten years before, and within three years used as custom-houses—we made our way to the broad main street. This is lined on each side by large, handsome shops, one or two banks, the new post-office in course of erection, and the large square town-hall, also unfinished. Then follow the new custom-house, land office, Canada Pacific Railway offices (square white brick buildings), and the round turret-like bastions of Fort Garry,* with its massive wooden palisades, and low log buildings at the extreme end of the street, where it terminates at the mouth of the Assiniboine. We had to cross a few yards of prairie in order to reach Mrs. T——'s house, formerly the officers' quarters of the mounted police force, now removed to Battleford and Fort McLeod. We were received very cordially, a welcome being extended to me, although a total stranger.

The first thing that struck me in Winnipeg was the mud. I had heard that Red River mud was the worst in the world, and I now for the first time realized how bad mud could be. Not only was the roadway so soft that every turn of a wheel loaded

---

* Fort Garry stands at the confluence of the Assineboine with the Red River.

it inches deep with the sticky compound, and made it so heavy that the driver had frequently to stop and clear his wheels with a stick, but, trodden from the crossings on to the side-walks, it covered them with a slimy mixture very difficult to walk on. From the windows I could see people slipping, sliding about so much, that any one ignorant of the cause might have attributed their unsteadiness to the strength of their morning libations; the absence of women from the streets making that solution appear possible if not probable.

On Sunday we went to Holy Trinity Church, a pretty little frame building with a full congregation. Part of the church was occupied by the regiment of artillery quartered in Fort Osborne, a neat little barracks to the west of the prairie. The choir was passable, and could boast of one thoroughly good tenor. An energetic clergyman preached an excellent sermon.

Towards the end of June, Mr. C——and his party left for the line; and we, having taken the house vacated by the T——s the week before, were busy getting comfortably settled. Numbers of people called; many of them old friends whom we had lost sight of for years; and every one was so cordial and friendly, that we anticipated great pleasure during our stay in Winnipeg.

It is a strange place, peopled with a strange variety from all quarters of the globe. Tall Indians stand in groups at the street corners, wrapped in long dirty-white, dark-blue, or scarlet blankets, held well about their shoulders, and hanging below their knees. They wear beaded or embroidered cloth leggings, blue, scarlet, or black, tied with gay ribbons. Their feet are in moccasins, their long black hair is braided with beads or ribbons, and a black silk handerchief, in which either feathers or a bunch of ribbons are fastened, is folded and knotted round their foreheads. Young squaws with shaggy, flowing hair, short, coloured merino skirts, and shawls over their heads, sit on the side-walks, chattering in their guttural tongue, and laughing over some joke; fat, glossy, half-breed ponies, in gorgeously beaded saddle-cloths, stand at the edge of the road awaiting their masters —short, lithe, dark men, who seem to touch the reins, vault into the saddle, and reach the end of the street in the same instant. The speed and strength of these small horses is wonderful; their glossy coats and well kept manes testify to the care taken of them. An Indian never beats his horse, nor drags at the reins in the cruel way so common among more "civilized" riders, but sits his horse as though it were part of himself. A long train of ox-carts is waiting to be loaded for the distant prairie hamlets. The half-breed driver stands by in trousers and checked shirt, a loosely knotted handkerchief about his neck. He sometimes wears a hat, but oftener his short, shaggy black hair is his only head-covering. His squaw sits in the bottom of the waggon; his little brown papooses are peeping out from between the bars at the side. Other children, laced up in queer, birch-bark cradles, or moss bags, leaving only their arms free, and the upper part of their bodies visible, lean against shop-doors or scattered bales of goods.

I watched some Indians shopping, and was astonished to see how invariably they waived aside inferior goods and chose such materials as merinos at a dollar and a half to two dollars a yard. One of the merchants told me it was useless to offer them anything but the best. An Indian who could not speak English or French, and wanted five things, divided his money according to his idea of their relative cost in little piles on the counter, and going through a pantomime descriptive of his wants, was handed first some silk handkerchiefs. Taking one up, he felt it, held it up to the light, and throwing it aside, shook his head vigorously, uttering an "Ugh!" of disgust. When shown a better one he was doubtful, but upon a much superior article being produced he took it, and willingly handed over one pile for it. This, however, was too much, and when given the change, he put it on one of the other piles, and proceeded in the same way to make the rest of his purchases.

"How easily they could be cheated!" I said to the clerk after the Indian had left.

"No," he replied, "not so easily as would appear. They generally come in from their camps in great numbers about once a year to sell their furs and make purchases. They go to different shops, and on their return compare notes as to the quality and cost of their goods. Then, if one has paid more than another, or has been cheated in quality, he will never enter the shop again, and the firm that gives the greatest bargains is most patronized on their return."

A few minutes later another Indian came to buy a blanket, and was told to go upstairs where they were kept. Slowly and doubtfully he ascended, feeling his way step by step, and holding closely to the banisters till he reached the top; then he turned to look back and express his astonishment in the "Ugh!" which, in different accents, means so many different things.

The Mennonites and Icelanders interested me very much. The former, who are all thrifty and energetic, make excellent settlers. They have a large settlement some twenty miles south-east of Winnipeg. The dress of the women is quaint, yet neat. They wear short, full skirts, just showing their small feet; jackets, and becoming white caps, from under which their round black eyes, small straight features, and intelligent expression, greet one pleasantly. The men are taller, with a quiet, unconscious air of superiority which is refreshing.

The dress of the Icelander is somewhat similar, but they are more lethargic-looking. They have bright "milk and roses" complexions, great opaque blue eyes, and a heavy gait that gives them an appearance of stupidity, which is not a true index of their character; they learn English rapidly, and are teachable servants, neat, clean, and careful, but have not constitutional strength to endure hard work, and when separated from their friends become lonely and dispirited. There is a large settlement of them at Gimli, about sixty miles from Winnipeg, on Lake Winnipeg. Some of the authorities in Winnipeg told me that, as an emigration speculation, they were not a success. The grass-hopper plague which visited Manitoba during two consecutive seasons destroyed their crops, and the ravages of small-pox during the fall of '76 and spring of '77 told upon them so severely that they have so far only been an expense to the Canadian Government.

The Hudson Bay Company's store had a great attraction for me. It was a long, low building within the precincts of Fort Garry, stocked with everything either useful or ornamental from a ship's anchor to a lace pocket-handkerchief; a sort of curiosity shop of all the necessaries and luxuries of life; an outfitting establishment where one could not only clothe oneself from head to foot, but furnish one's house from attic to cellar, at very reasonable prices. Whatever the charges may be at the outlying posts, competition keeps them within bounds in Winnipeg. As a rule the goods are excellent in quality, and to judge by the number of carts, carriages, and saddle-horses always grouped about the door of the store, a thriving business is done there.

The Red River at Winnipeg is much wider than at any other point, yet so high are the banks, that until quite close to it one cannot see the water. On the opposite or western shore is St. Boniface, the terminus of the branch line from Selkirk, and the site of the Roman Catholic cathedral, convents, and schools. The cathedral, a large square building, has a musical chime of bells, and the ringing of the "angelus," whose sound floated over the prairie unmarred by steam whistles, factory bells, or any other of the multitudinous sounds of a large city, was always welcome. Nowhere is evening more beautiful than in Manitoba. One instance in particular I noticed. The sun was setting low down in the heavens as in a sea of gold, one long flame-coloured line alone marking the horizon. In the south-west rose cloud upon cloud of crimson and gold, crossed by rapid flashes of pale yellow and white lightning, which momentarily obliterate their rich colours. To the south was a great bank of black thunder-cloud crested with crimson, reft to its deepest darkness by successive flashes of forked lightning. Immediately overhead a narrow curtain of leaden clouds was driven hither and thither by uncertain winds; while below, the prairie and all its varied life lay bathed in the warmth and light of the departing sun, throwing into bold relief the Indian wigwam, with its ragged sides and cross-poles.

Squaws were seated round the camp fires, or dipping water from a pool hard by; Indians were standing idly about; droves of cattle were being driven in for milking; groups of horses, their fore feet tied loosely together, were hobbling awkwardly as they grazed; tired oxen were tethered near, feeding after their day's work, while their driver lay under his cart and smoked. Above the low squat tent of the half-breed, there rose the brown-roofed barracks, its lazy flag clinging to the staff. Through the surrounding bushes water gleamed here and there. In the distance could be seen long trains of ox-carts, coming from remote settlements, the low monotonous moan of their ungreased wheels making a weird accompaniment to the muttering thunder; or a black-robed procession of nuns, on their way to the small chapel on the prairie, whose tinkling bell was calling them to prayers. An Indian on his fiery little steed, his beaded saddle-cloth glistening in the sun, was galloping in mad haste over the grass, away to the low hills to the north, which deserved their name of Silver Heights as they received the sun's good-night kiss.

Then the clouds, losing their borrowed tints, closed in like a pall; the low wail of the wind grew louder as it approached and swept them away to the south, leaving night to settle down upon the dwellers of the prairie city, starlit and calm, while the distant glow of the prairie fires rose luridly against the eastern sky. But all night long the creaking moan of the ox-carts went on, giving the prairie a yet closer resemblance to "an inland sea."

CHAPTER V.

Summer Days—The English Cathedral—Icelandic Emigrants—*Tableaux*—In chase of our Dinner—The Indian Summer—Blocked up—Gigantic Vegetables—Fruitfulness of the Country—Iceland Maidens—Rates of Wages—Society at Winnipeg—Half-breeds—Magic of the Red River Water—A Happy Hunting-ground—Where is Manitoba?

THE summer passed uneventfully. Day after day we watched for the white-covered mail-waggon, pails dangling underneath it, dogs trotting behind, rousing as they passed countless wild brethren from every quarter of the prairie. At sight of the waggon, we put on our hats and went to the post-office for letters from home; then drove across the prairie to Silver Heights, or down to the English Cathedral, which stood on the fairest bend of the river, and in a pretty, wooded dell—but, alas, it was encircled by a tangled, uncared-for churchyard, overgrown with weeds and thistles, the tombstones broken and prostrate, the fences so dilapidated that stray cattle leaped over them and grazed amongst the unrecognised graves. I was told that arrangements had been made for a city cemetery on the prairie, but the ground was merely staked off. A man who asked his way there was directed to go straight across the prairie to the east, until he came to where grass and sky met. Forgetting that as he advanced the horizon receded, he thanked his informant and went on his fruitless search; but after wandering many hours, like the boy after the pot of gold at the end of the rainbow, he returned weary and unsuccessful.

At the cathedral we heard the chorister boys chant the evening psalms; then went on to the little village of Kildonan, standing among green fields and thriving farms; or turned in another direction across the Assineboine, up a lovely road leading for miles through the woods. One morning we went to the emigrant sheds to see several hundred Icelanders embark in their flat-bottomed boats, with their quaint wooden chests, on their way to Gimli. On another occasion we helped to organize a Sunday-school festival, and after giving the children an unlimited supply of cake, strawberries, and lemonade, we amused them with some *tableaux*. Taking possession of a disused old church, we made an *impromptu* stage; by laying boards across the chancel railings; and the effect was so good, that some play-loving people enlarged on our idea by putting up rough side-scenes, and giving a series of entertainments the following winter, with the average amount of amateur skill.

One very hot Sunday, when we were without a servant, I rashly left our joint of roast beef on the kitchen table, while we discussed the pudding. Suddenly an ominous noise was heard. "Oh, Miss F—— !" exclaimed my hostess, starting up, "Do stop that dog! The wretch has stolen the beef—*all* to-morrow's dinner!"

To rush out of the house and over the prairie after the brute was the work of an instant; not so to catch him. On I ran, urged to redoubled exertions by Mrs. C——, who pursued me, excitedly flourishing her table napkin, while her little girl scrambled after her, screaming at being left behind. Every now and then the dog would stop to take breath, sitting still with aggravating coolness till I almost touched him, when off he would start again at redoubled speed. At last, after wildly throwing two or three handfuls of stones at him and all the sticks I could pick up as I passed, I aimed furiously at the barracks and hit the dog on the head, when he dropped the beef, and I returned hot and breathless, but triumphant.

The days were sultry, but the nights cool enough to make a blanket necessary, except just before the frequent thunderstorms. Well might the Indians call the Province "Manitoba" (God speaking), in their awe of the Great Spirit whose voice alone is so terrible. October is the most beautiful month in that region, bright, clear and balmy—the true Indian summer, with cool, dewy nights, when the aurora sent its long streaks of white and red light from the horizon to the zenith, to fall again in a shower of sparks, each night more beautiful than the last. Till, early in November, a storm of rain, succeeded by snow and frost, ended our Indian summer, and in forty-eight hours we had winter. Not weeks of slushy snow, changeable temperature, chilling rains, and foggy skies, as in Ontario, but cold, frosty, bracing winter at once. By the end of November the river was blocked, the boats had stopped running, and our only communication with the outside world was by means of the daily stage. But the wretchedness of a journey over the prairie to the nearest railway station was only encountered by those whose business made it unavoidable.

Before navigation had quite ceased, a provincial exhibition of the agricultural and other products of the country was held in the town-hall. Many of the vegetables were so large, that a description of them was treated with incredulity until some specimens were sent to Ottawa, to be modelled for the Philadelphian Centennial Exhibition. One Swedish turnip weighed over thirty-six pounds; some potatoes (early rose and white) measured nine inches long and seven in circumference; radishes were a foot and a half long and four inches round; kail branched out to the size of a currant bush; cabbages, hard, white, and good, grew to a foot and a half in diameter, and there were cauliflowers as large. Neither Indian corn, melons, nor tomatoes were exhibited, chiefly because most of the farmers in Manitoba have cultivated wheat-growing rather than market-gardening, as the former brings in the largest returns for the least labour.

Corn is grown in Manitoba larger and far taller than any I saw in Ontario. Tomatoes will grow in profusion in a dry spot, especially where, as in Keewatin, a hundred miles from Winnipeg, a southern exposure on sandy soil can be found; the same may be said of melons. Fruit trees are most difficult to cultivate, the frosts being so severe. Yet with care that obstacle may be overcome, and a few apples, grown and ripened in Mr. Bannatyne's garden, in Winnipeg, were exhibited. Every other kind of garden and farm produce was shown in abundance. The prairie soil is so rich that it yields a hundredfold, and the absence of the great preliminary labour of "clearing," which the early settlers in Ontario had to contend with, renders it a most advantageous country for emigrants. The chief difficulty is the scarcity of labour. All men not going out to take up land for themselves are employed on the railway; and women either are married and obliged to work on the farms with their husbands, or get married before they have been long in Manitoba. Many were the complaints I heard from people who had taken out female servants, paying their expenses and giving them high wages, only to lose them before they had been a month in the province. Their sole resource then was to employ Icelanders, who often could not speak a word of English, so that all directions had to be given by pantomime. Any one seeing the strange gesticulations and frantic efforts of some of the more energetic mistresses might be excused for thinking himself let loose in a city of lunatics.

Mrs. C—— had one of these Icelanders as nursemaid, and she did very well, picking up enough English in a few weeks to understand all we wanted. But I noticed that, however quickly she walked about the rest of the house, the stairs were as carefully traversed as though she had been an Indian. One day, hearing her in great distress on the kitchen stairs, I went to see what was the matter. The staircase was a narrow one between two walls, but without banisters; on the third or fourth step from the top sat one of the children, aged four years, and a few steps below stood the maid clinging to the smooth wall, her face white with terror, as, whenever she attempted to advance, the child made a feint to oppose her passage and push her back. Afraid either to turn round or retreat backwards, she stood trembling and calling for help, and it was impossible to avoid feeling amused at the absurdity of that big girl being intimidated by such a mite—who, with the original depravity of human nature, was enjoying the fun.

A friend of mine went through some odd experiences with these Iceland maids. Upon the arrival of a fresh domestic she was ordered to wash down the hall and door-steps. Next day, at the same hour, while a party of visitors were in the drawing-room, the door burst open, and Christian, scrubbing-pail and brush in hand, plumped down on her knees in the middle of the floor, and went through a vigorous pantomine of scrubbing. Her mistress was too astonished to speak for a moment or two, until the girl, surprised at her silence, looked up, uttering an indescribable " Eh?" of anxious inquiry, which was well-nigh too much for the gravity of her listeners.

Often, after ten minutes' patient endeavour to explain something, one was rewarded by a long drawn out " Ma'arum ?" infinitely trying to one's patience. Yet, in time, they often make excellent servants, and many people prefer them to Ontario or English emigrants. And certainly in point of economy they are infinitely superior to both; for not only will an Iceland maid waste nothing, but she is content with five or six dollars a month in wages, while girls from Ontario or England expect nine or ten dollars. Servants taken out on the line of railway demand and receive from fifteen to thirty dollars a month. These exorbitant wages are, however, lessening as immigration increases.

Society at Winnipeg is very pleasant; composed chiefly of the old families who formed the Hudson Bay Company and their descendants, many of whom have Indian blood in their veins. Their education, carefully begun by their parents, is often completed in Scotland, and they are well-read, intelligent people, as proud of their Indian as of their European descent. Many of them are handsome and *distingué*-looking. Their elegant appearance sometimes leads to awkward mistakes. One of these ladies, meeting a young Englishman fresh from the old country, and full of its prejudices, was entertained by him with reflections on race, and condolences at having to associate with half-castes. At last he inquired how long she had been in the country? Making him a stately curtsy, she answered—

"All my life! *I* am one of these despised half-breeds," and instantly left him. She said afterwards she was sorry for the poor fellow's discomfiture; but he brought it upon himself by disregarding all her efforts to change the conversation.

When the younger sons of good families are sent to seek their fortunes in the New World, their social standing is not fixed by their occupation, and a man who has served behind a counter all day is as well received in a drawing-room as one who has sat on the bench or pleaded a case in court. Of course in such a state of society impostors often effect an entrance, and their detection makes their entertainers chary of strangers afterwards. But so long as a man behaves himself like a gentleman he is treated as one. Many officials sent by the Canadian Government temporarily to fill responsible posts, and officers whose regiments have been disbanded, remain in Winnipeg, preferring it to any other part of Canada and illustrating the adage, " He who once drinks of the Red River water cannot live without it." It is a very muddy stream, however, and not at all inviting as a beverage.

A great many visitors, chiefly Englishman, go to Manitoba for the shooting and fishing, which are excellent. A friend of mine last year bagged four hundred ducks, several geese, great numbers of partridges, loons, and as many hares as he would waste shot on in a fortnight's holiday. No doubt, when Manitoba and its capabilities become better understood, and the line of railway is completed, the number of tourists in search of sport will much increase.

How little the new province has been known hitherto the following fact will show. A letter for me, mailed in a county town in England, in September, and merely addressed to Winnipeg, Manitoba, omitting Canada, travelled to France, where it received sundry postmarks, and such sensible hints by the post-office officials as, " Try Calcutta." At last, some one better acquainted with the geography of this side of the globe added, " Nouvelle Amerique," and my letter reached me, *viâ* New York, in Christmas week, richly ornamented with postmarks, and protests from officials that it " came to them in that condition;" tied together with two varieties of string; and frankly exhibiting its contents—a pair of lace sleeves, which, but for the honesty of the mail service, might easily have been abstracted.

CHAPTER VI.

Winter Amusements—A Winnipeg Ball—Forty Degrees below Zero—New Year's Day—" Saskatchewan Taylor "—Indian Compliments—A Dog-train—Lost in the Snow—Amateur Theatricals—Sir Walter Raleigh's Hat—A Race with the Freshets—The Ice moves!—The First Steamer of the Season—Good-bye to Winnipeg.

SNOW lay several inches thick on the ground at Christmas, and we had sleigh-drives over the smooth white prairie; one great advantage of Manitoban winters being that when once the ground is covered with snow, if only to the depth of five or six inches, it remains, and there is good sleighing until the frost breaks up in March or April. Sleighing parties are varied by skating at the rink and assemblies in the town-hall, where we meet a medley of ball-goers and givers, each indulging his or her favourite style of dancing—from the old-fashioned "three-step" waltz preferred by the elders, to the breathless "German," the simple *deux-temps*, and the graceful "Boston" dance, peculiar as yet to Americans and Canadians. The band was composed of trained musicians who had belonged to various regiments, and, on receiving their discharge, remained in Canada. The hall was well lighted, the floor in good condition, and we enjoyed taking a turn upon it, as well as watching the Scotch reels, country dances, and Red River jigs performed by the others.

It was a gay and amusing scene, but the heavy winter dresses—many of them short walking costumes—worn by the Manitoban belles, looked less pretty than the light materials, bright colours, and floating trains of an ordinary ball-room. The absence of carriages and cabs, and the intensity of the cold, compelled ladies to adopt this sombre attire. The mercury averaged from ten to twenty degrees below zero, frequently going as low thirty-three, and occasionally into the forties; yet the air is so dry and still, that I felt the cold less when it was thirty-three degrees below zero in Winnipeg than when only five degrees below in Ottawa, and did not require any additional wraps.

On New Year's Day the now old-fashioned custom

of gentlemen calling was kept up, and we had many visitors, among them the American Consul, Mr. Taylor, known in the Consulate as "Saskatchewan Taylor," from his interest in the North-West and anxiety upon all occasions to bring its capabilities before the public. He came in the evening, and, following the American style, remained more than an hour, so that we were able to get beyond the conventional topics of health and weather, and found him very pleasant and entertaining.

During the afternoon the maid came in, looking rather flurried, and said that visitors in the kitchen wished to see us. Going there, we were greeted by seven Indians and their squaws, come to pay a New Year's visit. As I looked at their brown faces and long, loose hair, memories of stories told by cousins in the Hudson Bay Company's service, of having to kiss all the squaws on New Year's Day, sent the blood with a rush back to my heart; but, happily, this ceremony was dispensed with. Only one of the party could speak English—a handsome, clear-skinned, straight-featured Indian, in blue blanket coat, red sash, leggings, and gaily-decorated hat. He stepped forward and made a little speech, wishing us "A long life of many moons, sunshine, health, and rich possessions, and the smile of the Good Spirit upon the blue-eyed papoose;" finishing by shaking hands all round. The others, with an "Ugh!" of acquiescence, and smiling faces, followed his example. Our hostess was unable to give them wine or whisky, because of the stringent prohibitory laws, but she regaled them on great slices of cake, with which they were much pleased. When Mr. C—— came in from the line with his dog-train—four strong beasts drawing a light cariole or covered tobogan, more like a great shoe than anything else—the blue and red coat of his Indian runner, Tommy Harper, was much admired by our visitors; and he told us afterwards of their admiration for everything they saw in the house. This Tommy was a good-tempered old fellow, but, when not running, was invariably asleep or smoking over the kitchen fire.

About the middle of January (1877) we had a terrible snow-storm, the worst that had been known in Manitoba for years. At five o'clock in the evening the wind rose suddenly, and in half an hour was blowing a gale, sending the snow whirling through the air in such blinding volume, that it was impossible to distinguish anything twenty yards off. As night closed in, which it does early at that season, the storm increased in violence, and, although there was then little snow falling, the wind drove in all directions the dry snow lying upon the ground.

Many people lost their way. A shop-boy running home to tea, only round the corner of the block, missed the turning into the gateway, and wandered till daylight on the prairie, knowing it was certain death to lie down. A family crossing the prairie, and seeing the storm approaching, hastened to reach a wayside inn four or five hundred yards distant, but before they could do so lost sight of it. After driving several hours they were obliged to stop; and digging a hole in the snow with their hands, covered themselves with robes and sleigh-rugs, and drawing the sleigh over them as a little protection from the wind, they waited until daylight—to find themselves within a hundred yards from the inn! All next day stories were continually reaching us of narrow escapes, of frozen feet and hands, of lost horses, frozen oxen, and travellers' miseries in general. But this certainly was an exceptional storm, or " blizzard," as the natives say.

Towards the end of winter it was proposed that some *tableaux* should be exhibited in the town-hall for the benefit of a local charity. The suggestion was hailed with delight, and every one likely to be useful was invited to "talk it over" with Mrs. C——. And talk they did, at such length and with such vivacity, that I wondered how the two stage-managers, Captain H—— and Miss P——, could ever evolve order from such a chaos. The great clatter of tongues in that small room reminded me of an old Scotch nurse of ours, who, being summoned to keep house for a minister cousin, was anxious first to learn how to play the lady and entertain her guests. The cook advised her to listen at the drawing-room door when we had a party: but she quitted her post in disgust, having heard nothing but "a muckle clackit."

At last it was settled that the *tableaux* were to represent the story of " Beauty and the Beast," " Elizabeth knighting Raleigh," scenes from " Hamlet" and "The Bohemian Girl," an emblematic group of the nations included in the British Empire, surrounded by representatives of the army and navy, and some well-known statues. Assuredly there was variety enough in our programme to suit all tastes!

Our dress rehearsal, held in the old church before mentioned, was more amusing—to the actors, at all events—than the performance itself. The "sides," which looked well enough to those without, proved a delusion and a snare to those within. They were used as dressing-rooms, but their partition from the stage being only partial, and their flooring stopping far short of the front, a great gap was left—a pitfall down which everything tumbled. Their appointments were primitive, consisting of a small looking-glass, a pincushion, and a piece of comb in each room. The "properties" on the ladies' side were an old straw bonnet wreathed with artificial flowers, and a gaudy overskirt; and on that of the gentlemen, two hats, and a pistol and tin mug—which had probably done duty for the "dagger and the bowl," in the last scene of a dreadful tragedy. Some of our amateurs were fortunate enough to get complete costumes made, but others appeared in a fragmentary condition, with a bodice of the time of Elizabeth, and a petticoat of that of Victoria. Sir Walter Raleigh wore the old felt hat belonging to his dressing-room, and pathetically appealed to the spectators to imagine it adorned with a white feather and jewelled clasp.

The girls who appeared in more than one scene had to change their dresses, and it is impossible to describe the confusion of belongings then thrown in a vast heap on the floor, or the despair of one young performer whose polonaise had disappeared in the gulf. As all were in different stages of *déshabille*, no gentleman could be called to the rescue; so I lay down on my face and groped about with my hands till I fished it up. But before I succeeded, two or three people were standing on my skirts, and a pile of gipsy costumes was deposited on my legs. My rising sent dismay to the owners' hearts, and they wailed that they would "never be able to find their things again!"

When the great night arrived we, by means of jewellery constructed of gold paper and glass buttons, and other ingenious devices, made a brilliant show, and the general effect was pronounced excellent. We had crowded houses for two consecutive nights, and the only drawback to the pleasure of our *tableaux* was the sad and sudden death of one of Captain H——'s children, which took place on the first night, and aroused general sympathy.

Soon after our theatrical entertainments the snow almost entirely disappeared, cricket was played on the prairie, and people began to look forward to the reopening of navigation, and to bet actively on the day and hour when the first steamboat would arrive; though the ice was still so solid that horse-races were held on the river.

The 25th of April was a warm day, succeeding heavy rains, and it was hoped that the ice would move next day. In the evening we were at an assembly in the town-hall, which is built on the side of a broad, shallow *coulée* or gully. About ten o'clock, seeing several people look anxiously from the windows, we went to inquire the cause, and found the "water was out." Freshets from the prairies were rushing down the *coulée* beneath, carrying everything before them—dog-kennels, logs, broken furniture, boxes, and all the usual *debris* found scattered about the houses on the prairie. The freshets increased so rapidly, that it was feared if we did not leave at once we should never get home, the water being level with the bridge, which was in imminent danger of being carried away. The lower story of the hall was also flooded, and considered scarcely safe. So there was cloaking in hot haste, and the gentlemen who lived near brought all the top-boots and goloshes they could collect for the benefit of those who had to cross the partially submerged roads.

The ice did move next day, and on the 27th, at the sound of the steamboat whistle, I ran to the window. As if by one impulse, every door on the main street opened, and the inmates poured forth, men putting on their coats, women their bonnets, while holding the kicking, struggling bare-headed babies they had snatched up in their haste to reach the landing as soon as the boat; boys of all sizes, ages, and descriptions, gentle and simple, rich and poor, mustered as though by magic. In five minutes the streets and banks of the river were black with people rushing to meet the steamer, and the shout that greeted her at the wharf was loud and genuine. It was the last time her arrival caused such excitement, as before another season the railway was running to St. Boniface, and freight and passengers could get to Winnipeg all through the winter.

The spring of 1877 was wet and backward, and we looked forward to our journey out to the contract, where a house was nearly ready for us, with anything but unmixed pleasure. In the hope that the state of the roads might improve, we delayed our departure until the first week in June. For my own part, I rejoiced over every additional delay, as I was loth to leave Winnipeg, and the many kind friends I had made there.

CHAPTER VII.

A Manitoban Travelling-carriage—The Perils of Short Cuts—The Slough of Despond—Paddy to the Rescue!—"Stick-in-the-Mud" and his Troubles—McQuade's—An Irish Welcome—Wretched Wanderers.

AFTER many days of packing, general confusion, and disturbing dust, culminating in breakfast in the kitchen, dinner on a packing-case in the parlour, high tea at a neighbour's in our travelling-gear, and a night at the hotel, we rose at five o'clock on the morning of the 5th of June to be ready for our journey to Clear Water Bay. All the teams, with the household goods and chattels, had started the day before, except two for personal baggage, and the one we were to occupy.

Of course we were ready too soon, and hours were spent in standing idly about, and going to the gate to see if the teams were coming. When they were at last packed and off, it was decided to be altogether too late for us to follow until after luncheon, which, with only an uncertain prospect of a heavier meal later, we turned into dinner. Then some one remembered half a dozen forgotten things, which it was impossible to do without, and it was nearly four o'clock when our waggon arrived—a springless vehicle with three narrow seats, and drawn by two broken-winded steeds.

After packing all our *impedimenta* in the waggon, there was literally no room for us. What was to be done? Between our efforts to make the driver, a stupid, tipsy French half-breed, understand English by screaming it as loud as we could, the variety of our baggage, and the curiosity of the passers-by, we soon had a small crowd of interested listeners and apparently sympathizing friends. Finally the livery stable keeper made his appearance, and after some discussion agreed to exchange that waggon for a larger one. Jumping into it, he lashed the horses, who went at a furious pace down the street, proving their powers, but, alas, scattering the half-packed contents of the waggon—rugs, cushions, blankets, tin kettles, and pails—at irregular intervals over the road. In half an hour a larger vehicle was brought, and we hastily repacked, receiving contributions of our property from every one who passed while the operation was going on, so that it was late in the afternoon before we left Winnipeg. When we arrived at the river, of course the ferry-boat was on the opposite side, and we had to wait for its return, which seemed the climax to the day's worries. We growled audibly, feeling that we were entitled to do so, having had enough provocation to ruffle the most angelic tempers. With scarcely room to sit, and nowhere, to speak of, to put our feet, bodily discomfort helped to put us out of humour.

Can you imagine a three-seated waggon, containing a load of valises, travelling-bags, a tin box of edibles for a week's journey, tents, blankets, pans, kettles, pails, a box of earth filled with bedding plants, a bundle of currant bush slips, a box of cats—being *the* cat and five kittens—a box of family silver, engineers' instruments, wraps of every description, provender for the horses, a bag of bread, the driver's own provisions (it was a part of the bargain that he was to "find." himself), loose articles of all kinds, thrown in at the last moment, five adults, two children, one small dog and an unhappy-looking canary? This motley assemblage was stowed away as well as possible, the kettles and pails being hung at the back and sides, after the fashion of the travelling tinkers' carts. There certainly was a very emigrant-like appearance about the whole thing, in spite of the tasteful trimming of our shade hats.

The ferry-boat came for us at last, and as we drove over the prairie at a moderate rate, delays having become things of the past, we were for the next hour almost merry. This transient joy was soon dispelled by our driver, who, without any warning, turned off the road through some swampy ground. Pulling up suddenly before an apparently unbroken line of trees, he craned his neck first one way and then the other in search of an opening, unheeding the expostulations in French and English with which he was assailed, until, finding what he sought, and flicking his whip over the horses' ears, he condescended to reply, "*Je fais le detour!* Bad, *voila!*" Then, urging his horses on, he charged into the bushes, and drove along what had been once a cart trail (one could hardly call it a road), overgrown with underbrush. Long branches met overhead, and we were kept busy, alternately warding them off our faces and holding on to our seats—for the track was a succession of uneven hills, hollows, and short turns, with which our driver seemed as unacquainted as ourselves.

About six o'clock we came to the high-road, which crossed the end of our track—the high-road that has cost our country nearly a million dollars—the far-famed and much-talked-of Dawson road. It was some two feet higher than our rough track, and separated from it by a large mud-puddle, in which, after a lurch to one side and a violent jerk from the horses, the waggon-wheels sunk on the other. A volley of oaths was discharged by our half-breed, followed by a crack of his long whip, and a sharp struggle, and then the near horse fell back on his haunches and we stuck fast. Down rolled the best valise, out sprang Jehu, carrying with him into the mud our biggest blanket. Mr. C——, in slippers, sat on the top of the waggon demanding his boots, which were *somewhere* at the bottom; somebody else was searching wildly for a rope and axe, which proved to be *nowhere;* everybody was giving a different opinion on the best means of extricating ourselves, only uniting in one thing, namely, abuse of the driver, who stood knee-deep in mud, hitching up his trousers and muttering something about *le détour.* We women, meantime, tried to quiet the screaming children, and prevent the "unconsidered trifles" which filled the corners of the waggon from falling out—a duty not unattended with danger, as pussy, on guard over her nursery, and excited by the general *bouleversement,* gave a spiteful claw to any foot or hand which approached near to her box.

No rope, axe, or chain, could be found; there was nothing but mud on every side to unload in, and not a house for miles to shelter us for the night. Fortunately, before very long a waggon passed on the high-road, whose occupants were a kindly Irishman, his wife, and child.

"Faith, is it help ye want, yer honour? It's meself never refused help to any man," said Paddy; and jumping down, he produced a chain. Fastening the pole of the waggon to one end, and the horses to the other, he drove them up to the high-road, where, having firmer foothold, a few pulls drew us out of the mud-hole. We thanked the old man for his help, but saw him and his chain depart with regret. Having better horses and a lighter load, he soon left us far behind.

On we jogged, sometimes on the road, but more often off it, driving through every clump of trees that grew in our way, as the roots gave some firmness to the swampy ground. Now and then, when returning to the road, the waggon would almost stick, but, after a lunge, pull, and a struggle, attended by a volley of French from our Jehu, and a screech from the women, it righted itself again. A little later we passed the teams that had left Winnipeg so long before us in the morning; one of them was stuck deep in the mud, and the drivers were just parting company—the first, a French Canadian, declining to help the second, an Irish Canadian boy, whose good-natured face was a picture of dismay, as he stood contemplating the scene of disaster. The Frenchman declared that he had stuck three times, and had to unload both teams twice, and he wasn't going to do it again; so he whipped up his horse and left poor young "Stick-in-the-Mud," as we dubbed him, to his fate. Promising to send a yoke of oxen from McQuade's, five miles further on, where we intended putting up for the night, we also left him, but not without regret. I could not help feeling sorry for the poor boy out there alone on the prairie, perhaps for the whole night, as it was by no means certain that the hoped-for yoke of oxen would be forthcoming. But the lad was so civil, and evidently so determined to make the best of things, that fortune favoured him. A mile further on we met a long train of carts, and Mr. C—— shouted to the driver of the first to go and help "Stick-in-the-Mud," promising to pay him for his services. By this time it was getting dark, the mosquitos were troublesome, and the children were hungry and cross, and we joyfully hailed the first glimmer of the lights at McQuade's. But though in sight of the haven where we would be, our troubles were not yet over. Crossing a broken culvert not half a mile from the house, one of the horses fell in, and we all had to get out and walk, an annoyance which we felt to be the "last straw" on our much-enduring backs.

McQuade's is merely a farm-house on the main road. But in the usual condition of those roads it is the first stopping-place from Winnipeg, and McQuade's or "Little Pointe du Chene," as it is sometimes called, is familiar to all the engineers on the staff of that part of the Canada Pacific Railway. The yard was full of the teams which had left Winnipeg the day before, and the kitchen, or general living room, was crowded with teamsters, who, however, when we appeared, withdrew to a dark little cook-house a few yards from the door.

The room vacated for us was low-roofed, with unplastered ceiling, whose rafters were hung with bunches of garden herbs. Two narrow windows were set sideways in the wall, their deep window-seats serving as bookcase and sideboard: holding the Bible and almanac, the old lady's best bonnet, a pot or two of preserves, a nose-gay of spring-flowers, and a tea-caddy. An old-fashioned four-post bedstead stood in one corner, covered with a patchwork quilt; in another was an impromptu bed, spread on the floor, and occupied by a woman and two children, apparently asleep. A table, covered with oil-

G

cloth, with some cups and saucers on it, stood between the bed and a dresser cupboard, containing rows of shining milk-pans, piled one on the top of the other and separated by a board. Behind the house door a flight of narrow steps led "up ter chamber," as the old woman in the rocking-chair informed us; and underneath these stairs was a primitive washing apparatus, consisting of a bench holding a basin and two wooden pails, with a long towel hanging from a stick.

The farmer bustled in and out, greeting some of us as old friends, summoning Alice, the maid-of-all-work—a down-trodden, stupid-looking girl of fourteen—to make up the fire and get the kettle boiling, and putting his head into the doorway, "just to tell missus," as he ushered us in. "The missus," a kindly-looking Irishwoman, in a white cap and kerchief, wriggled over in her chair to greet us, for she was "set fast by the rheumatism," and could not rise. But from long confinement in her chair she had learnt to get about in it very well; her natural energy expending itself on shuffling all over the room, screaming to Alice to know "why that there kettle didn't boil?" and generally making us welcome in her way.

"There's lots of milk—plenty; you are welcome to it, and there'll be boilin' water presently. If I could only get a holt of that Alice, I'd make things lively for her! I'm wore out with her intirely. If you've brought your own provisions, all right; but there have been so many travellers by lately, there isn't a bite in the house, till me eldest darter comes and bakes for me to-morrow." Yes, she had seven darters, all well married round about, blessed be God! and they came turn and turn about to look after the old people, do the work, and see after things, while she just kept the bit thing Alice to do the chores and wait on her; but she warn't much good.

Thus our hostess ran on, until the horse was extricated, and we got possession of our rugs and provisions. The boiling water appearing at the same time, we soon sat down to tea; and, as it was too late to pitch our tent that night, we spread our rugs and blankets on the two bedsteads "up ter chamber"—a mere unfurnished garret—and were soon in bed.

Not long afterwards, hearing a great deal of laughter downstairs, I listened, and gathered that "Stick-in-the-Mud" had arrived, and the men were chaffing him for having paid the half-breed two dollars for lending him two oxen for five minutes to extricate his train.

Tired as I was, the mosquitos were so attentive that I found it impossible to sleep. About midnight "that wretched Alice" crept up the stairs, and lay down in a corner, partitioned off from the rest of the garret by a grey blanket nailed to the rafters. I am sure she did not undress much, nor could she have slept long, as she was downstairs again before three o'clock, and I heard the old woman rating her from her bed.

When we descended at about six, the men and teams were all gone, and the tenants of the floor bed had taken advantage of an offered ride to help them on their way. Poor woman! she was journeying from Detroit, to the work on "15," to join her brother. She had been a month on the road, and had still another week or ten days of walking before her.

CHAPTER VIII.

Faithless Jehu—The "Blarney Stone"—Mennonites in search of News—"Water, Water everywhere"—A Herd of Buffaloes—A Mud Village—Pointe du Chêne and Old Nile—At Dawson Route—A Cheerful Party—*Toujours perdrix*—The "Best Room"—A Government Shanty—Cats and Dogs—Birch River—Mushroom-picking—The Mosquito Plague—A Corduroy Road—The Cariboo Muskeg.

WHEN we resumed our journey, the weather was hazy and seemed to threaten a thunderstorm. Accordingly, we made great haste, in the hope of reaching "Pointe du Chêne" proper before the storm broke. But when all else was ready, neither our Jehu nor his steeds could be found; he had taken them about a mile further on, to spend the night at a friend's, and did not make his appearance until eight o'clock. As I bade our old hostess goodbye, she seized hold of my ulster, and feeling its texture, said—

"Are you warm enough, child, in that thing? Ye'll feel the cold drivin'. Ye'd better have a shawl."

Thanking her for her inquiries, I assured her that I was quite warm.

"Ah, well," she said, patting me on the arm; "take care of yourself. Good people are scarce."

Poor old creature! her good nature made me glad she was my countrywoman. A kind thought expressed in the familiar accents of "Ould Oireland" is welcome to the wayfarer in strange lands, even though it may often be "only blarney" after all.

Reaching a bend in the little river Seine at noon, we halted for dinner, and lighted a fire. But not daring to waste much time in unpacking, we took what we could eat in our fingers, and fed the children. Before we had finished, we were joined by a party of Mennonites, in a comfortable covered waggon drawn by two powerful horses. The family consisted of an elderly man; his wife, a pretty, quaint-looking little woman; a daughter, apparently sixteen; a boy of twelve; and two little girls of about six, looking like twins. They were well dressed, in the quaint costume of their country. The man, who alone could speak English, told us they were going to Winnipeg to hear the war news, and gave a look of utter astonishment at our ignorance of the latest telegrams. It made me feel quite ashamed of not having taken more interest in the progress of current events, to meet a party of emigrants driving miles through these solitudes to hear what I had passed heedlessly by when close under my hand. The Mennonite elder was very polite; but, judging from the shrugs indulged in by the family after a remark uttered in their own language, they did not think highly of our intelligence.

Before we were packed into the waggon again the rain came down in earnest, and the whole afternoon was spent in vain endeavours to keep ourselves dry. Waterproofs, blankets, umbrellas, all were soaked, as hour after hour we were dragged slowly through the muskeg, or marsh, following no apparent track, and with the water often up to the "hubs" of the wheels. No sooner were our umbrellas placed in a suitable position to keep off the rain, than Jehu would make one of his *détours*, and the wind and rain meeting us on the other side, away flew our wraps, and all the umbrellas had to be rearranged. The difficulty of doing this, and yet keeping them from dripping down some one's neck, was almost insuperable. Mosquitoes, too, flying about in swarms added their quota to our discomfort. The poor canary had a hard time of it, for in spite of all our care the cage repeatedly filled with water, which I had to empty over the side of the waggon. Luckily, the cats kept quiet, and no one was anxious to know whose feet were in the box of plants!

About three miles from Pointe du Chêne, a herd of buffalo feeding in the distance made us forget our misery for a moment. They had not been met with so near a civilized neighbourhood for years; the wet and stormy weather was the cause of their approach. I was disappointed in their appearance; they looked to me very like a herd of farm cattle, but seemed to feed closer together. I had, however, not much chance to study their peculiarities, another *détour* speedily requiring my attention. On looking for the buffaloes when again at leisure, they were nowhere to be seen.

Pointe du Chêne is, without exception, the muddiest village I ever was in. We drove through streams of mud; fences were built in mud; mud extended on every side for acres. The houses were so surrounded with mud; ankle-deep, nay, knee-deep, that one wondered how the inmates ever got out. Yet they told us that in a few weeks all would be quite dry; that what were now some of the largest mud-lakes would then be the finest wheat-fields; and it is possible that mud here may have the same fertilizing properties as it has on the banks of the Nile, and that agriculture may be carried on upon the same principles in this part of Canada as in Egypt.

At the Dawson route way-house we were received by a white-haired old man *en route* to take a situation as cook in one of the houses on the line—though certainly no one ever looked less like a cook. He ushered us into the kitchen, the only room boasting a fire, and we were there met by the proprietor, a depressed and apologetic sort of person. After several whispered consultations with a hopeless wife, who moved in melancholy protest, or sat with her head leaning against the wall, applying the corner of her apron to her eyes so constantly, that that particular corner would not lie flat when allowed to drop, he put up a stove in the front room, which was soon festooned in every direction with our drenched garments.

Two rooms upstairs, clean-looking, but almost devoid of furniture, were allotted to us, and finding that we should be unable to continue our journey for at least thirty-six hours, we tried to make the best of them. Fearing that we might encounter further delays where it would be impossible to get food, we decided to husband what we had, especially as we discovered that our Jehu, whenever he got into the waggon from the wet muskeg, had sat on the bag of bread, which still further reduced our supplies. Accordingly we determined to content ourselves with whatever might be set before us, which proved to be pork, bread, and tea for breakfast; bread, tea, and pork for dinner; and tea, pork, and bread for supper. As we ventured to make a mild remark upon the monotony of the bill of fare, a bottle of pickles was produced next morning, our dejected hostess informing us, in a sepulchral tone, that it cost " one dollar, Hudson Bay Company store prices."

Towards nightfall the French teamster arrived, with his load rather mixed. He had been compelled to unload and reload so often, that everything was where it should not be. Stove-pipes, down which the rain poured in rusty streams, were lying on the top of the best mattresses; and, generally speaking, all the light things were underneath, and all the heavy ones on the top. Soon after the Frenchman, "Stick-in-the-Mud" arrived alone, drenched and miserable. *His* load was again "stuck in the muskeg, a matter of two mile off, he guessed." If left there all night, it would sink so deep in that quicksand-like marsh that there would be little hope of ever extracting it. The poor lad said his team was too done up to be of any use, and he was so "dead tired, he hadn't a leg to stand on." Still, he didn't object to go back if men and teams were sent with him. And after a great deal of tramping through the muddy village, our people succeeded in getting a yoke of oxen to send to the rescue of our Saratogas.

Meantime the best room of the inn had been "tidied up"—I suppose in our honour, for next day our meals were served there instead of in the kitchen as at first. It resembled the "best room" of most Canadian farmhouses. A four-post bedstead stood in one corner, covered with a patchwork quilt, generally the work of the wife when a girl; a bureau was decorated with the few books possessed by the family—usually a Bible, almanac, and photograph album—the best cups and saucers, a looking-glass, and a pin-cushion; an old-fashioned roomy sofa filled another corner. The dining-table in the centre had extension leaves, very far from level; the wall was decorated with a big clock, a couple of bright-coloured prints, a portrait or two and a sampler; and the floor was covered in patches with rag mats.

If we flattered ourselves that promotion into the "best room" would ensure privacy, we were doomed to disappointment. The whole family, from the doleful mamma to the youngest olive-branch, favoured us with their presence, sat on the sofa, and, looking through the album, were kind enough to discuss their relations and friends *pro bono publico*. The youngest child, aged five, having an occasional inclination to lay violent hands upon portions of our dinner, was pounced upon by one or other of her family, roughly shaken or thumped, and banged down upon a hard wooden chair; while from some other loving relative came the remark, made between set teeth, "I'd slap her, I would!" Poor little thing! she did not seem " a' there," as the Scotch say; the frequent boxing and banging her poor head underwent probably increasing, if it did not occasion, her stupidity.

Early on Friday morning we set out again under more favourable auspices, though the day was cold and cloudy. One of the division superintendents, or " walking bosses " as they are called, employed by the contractors, had arrived at our resting-place the day before, *en route* for the " Angle," and he offered to exchange teams with us, if we would allow him to accompany his good horses. This proposal was gladly accepted, and with the utmost satisfaction we saw our French-Indian Jehu depart with his ill-conditioned brutes.

After leaving Pointe du Chêne, the road for some distance lies up a long rocky hill, and then passes through a comparatively well-wooded country. But we thought little of surrounding scenery. The wind was so cold, and the frequent snow-storms during the day were so disagreeable, that we had quite enough to do to keep ourselves and the children warm.

We had our dinner near a dismantled log-house on the bank of a narrow creek, and reaching Whitemouth River about seven, put up at a shanty built by Government to shelter travellers on the Dawson road. It is kept by a Norwegian named Nord and his wife, and can only boast of three small rooms and a kitchen. It was too cold to camp out, so, spreading our rugs and blankets on the floor, we lay down and slept, too tired to heed the hardness of the boards.

On Saturday the air was warmer, and the road comparatively good, and we were sufficiently at ease to look out for and admire the wild-flowers that grew on every side (Mr. R—— good-naturedly stopping to gather some for us), and watch for the young rabbits started by the dogs, who yelped loudly when in full chase after them. We had two dogs when we left Winnipeg, but now our pack numbered eight, some joining us at every halting-place. But in the same proportion that the dogs increased, the cats decreased, a kitten being begged at every house, as they were overrun with mice: and our cats were received with almost as much delight as Dick Whittington's historical speculation. Unfortunately, however, the recipients were too poor to make our fortunes in return.

At noon we passed our teamsters and Mr. R——'s gang of navvies, rather picturesquely grouped round their camp fire, where tea was boiling and pork frying. The untethered horses were feeding by the roadside, and "Stick-in-the-Mud," for once superior to his name, was alone plodding steadily on. This was our easiest day's journey, and it was scarcely four o'clock when we reached Birch River, a dry sandy hill round which a tiny creek wound. We were glad of a few hours' respite to run about and stretch our weary limbs. One of our party discovering that the banking of the shanty was full of mushrooms, we gathered a great many, and took them to the kitchen to be cooked.

This way-house is kept by two brothers, who have literally nothing to do but cook, eat, and sleep, bare shelter being all that the Government supplies to travellers. One of the brothers was making doughnuts and boiling them in a pot of fat, and although they did not look tempting I had the greatest curiosity to taste them. However, as he did not give me any encouragement to ask for one, my curiosity remained unsatisfied, and I had to content myself with the mushrooms, which had full justice done to them.

As night came on, the mosquitoes were terrible; smoke was of no avail to keep them away. The cook told me that the season for them was only just beginning, and that they were nothing to what they would be in a month. The previous summer their cow had literally been tortured to death, between the mosquitoes and deer flies. Mr. C—— had a mosquito netting tent which was put up in the room we slept in, so that we had comparative exemption from their torments; but it was too hot to sleep, and all night long I heard the men outside fighting with and swearing at their winged enemies.

We set out early on Sunday, as we had a long day's drive before us, and were to have our first experience of a corduroy road. The one in question was a very bad specimen, a succession of deep mudholes, round some of which we skirted cautiously, wondering how "Stick-in-the-Mud" would get through, and plunging into some swamps, which seemed to tax all the strength our team could exert to lug us out again. We soon arrived at the great Cariboo muskeg, on the smooth squared-timber road. This muskeg must, at some earlier stage of the world's existence, have been a great lake full of islands; now it is a grassy swamp, the water clear as spring water, studded with groups of high rocks of varied size and shape, overgrown by tall pines, birch, scrubby underbrush, ferns, and moss. We had been getting on with such comparative ease that we began to think our fears of the "corduroy road" had been groundless; but before night we experienced the wisdom of the warning not to "halloo before we were out of the bush." We took our lunch on some flat rocks, near a place known on the road as "six-mile shanty;" not without difficulty as the dogs, like ourselves, were hungry, and while we were in chase of a refractory umbrella carried away by the wind, one dog demolished the butter and another ran off with our roast of beef: and when we reflected that it was the last fresh meat we were likely to taste for months, we saw it depart with regret, even though the ham had been left us.

If the roads were bad in the morning, they were ten times worse in the afternoon; and nothing, I think, will ever make me forget the last five miles of real corduroy road we traversed before reaching the "Angle." It consisted of round logs, loosely bound together, and thrown down upon a marsh, no two consecutive logs being of the same size. There had originally been some foundation, and there were still deep drains dug on each side; but the logs had given way at different ends in some parts, and altogether in others. It was bump, bump, bang, and swash; swash, bang, and bump; now up, now down, now all on one side, now all on the other. Cushions, rugs, everything that could slide, slid off the seats; the children were frightened and fretting; the bird fluttered itself almost to death in vain attempts to escape; the kittens were restless; and all our hairpins, slipping down our backs, added a cold shiver to our other miseries.

One longed to cry out and beg to be allowed to stop, if only for a moment. But of what use would that have been? We had to endure it, so it was best to get it over quickly. In many places the old road was completely gone, and we had to drive through such dreadful holes that we wondered the waggon came out entire.* Never was smooth road greeted with greater pleasure than we hailed the last mile from the "Angle;" and never did more stiff and weary travellers arrive at any bourn than our party when alighting at the "Angle" that night.

---

* Much of this part of the road is now under water and well-nigh impassable, the prospect of soon having the Canada Pacific Railway in working order making it seem waste of time and money to repair it.

CHAPTER IX.

The "Nor'-west Angle"—The Company's House—Triumph of "Stick-in-the-Mud"—On the Lake of the Woods—A Gallant Cook—Buns à l'imprévu—A Man overboard!—Camping out—Clear Water Bay—Our First Portage—A Noble Savage—How Lake Rice and Lake Deception won their Names—At our Journey's End.

THE "Nor'-west Angle" is a little village at the north-west corner of the Lake of the Woods, and at the mouth of a nameless river, or narrow arm of the lake. The banks on one side are high and wooded, on the other high also, but completely bare of shrubs or trees; while between them the river wanders hither and thither through marshy ground, looking somewhat as one fancies the fens at home must do.

The company's house is a long, low white building, with narrow windows and doors, neat fences and grass plots in front, and a very fair kitchen garden, showing signs of care and attention. The houses near are all one-storied, log-built, and plastered with mud inside and out. There are also several birch-bark wigwams, full of smoke and swarthy children; the owners squatting at their low doors, or, with their dirty blankets wrapped more tightly round them, leaning on the fence to stare at the new-comers.

The "Angle" was quite lively that afternoon. All our own teams were there, "Stick-in-the-Mud" having arrived first after all, with his load in a better condition than the others. Such a genuine smile of satisfaction beamed on his good-natured face, that I could not forbear congratulating him on his triumph over difficulties. Several other teams had brought supplies for the contractor; and fifty or sixty navvies going out in search of work on the contract, were camped about everywhere; some in tents, some under waggons, while some sat up all night round the fires, smoking and recounting their experience of the road. Many of the men were very lame and stiff, after their hundred-mile tramp. Numbers of Indians had come in to trade, and the ceaseless "tom-tom" from the wigwam on the opposite bank told how they were gambling away their earnings. They kept up this dissipation until daylight, when they went away in canoes.

The way-house being full when we arrived, the Hudson Bay Company's officer very kindly vacated his quarters for us, and paid us every attention in his power, even robbing his tiny garden of half its early lettuce for our benefit. We had a comfortable night's sleep, much enjoyed after our toils and troubles, and on a misty summer morning we packed ourselves and our luggage into a large rowing-boat. The big steamer, *Lady of the Lake*, being, as usual, stuck on a rock, about forty miles out, we were towed behind a barge by a shaky looking little tug. Glad were we to have room to move about a little, and after the crowded and cramping waggon the boat seemed a paradise.

Floating almost due north over the smooth waters of the bay, we were soon on the Lake of the Woods. The scenery is very lovely; island follows island. Some seem but a pile of moss-covered stone, every crevice filled with ferns, blueberries, and wild juniper bushes; others are great masses of rock, their perpendicular sides covered with curling black cariboo moss and crowned with great pines; others, again, have shelving sandy shores, covered with tangled vines and bright-hued wild-flowers. As we passed along, each long stretch of the lake appeared more beautiful than the last. Then the sun went down, turning to gold and crimson the fleecy clouds mirrored in the lake, glinting on the distant white pines, throwing into bold relief their darker brothers and the jagged walls of moss-covered rock, in varied tints—black, red, green and white. The shadows slowly deepened, the long grey clouds hung like a curtain in the sky, where the stars began to gleam softly. The varied foliage turned to a deep, rich blue, shading into green like a peacock's tail. Silence was around us, broken only by the weird cry of the loon diving in the distant bay, and the ceaseless, monotonous puff-puff of the little tug as she pursued her way over the peaceful waters.

About three or four o'clock—how little note we took of time!—we reached the rock on which the big steamer was still fast, stopping to give her another anchor and cable, and wishing her good luck and a speedy release.

We had been amusing ourselves during the afternoon by watching the cook on the barge dive up and down through the narrow doorway of a sort of box, to a small, rusty, sheet-iron cooking-stove, with an equally rusty stove-pipe. First seizing an axe, he chopped up some wood from a pile in the corner, and filled the stove; then he dragged down a bag of flour into his den; then up again he started, as suddenly as a Jack-in-the-box, for a round tin; then for some flat pans. Next we heard him shouting from below, "Is that fire burning good, boys? Cram her full; pile in more wood, and don't heed the smoke!" and he suddenly appeared with the pans full of buns, which were quickly baked. Then, leaning over the railings of the barge, he cried—

"If you would have your tea now, ladies, while the buns are hot, and would pass along your tea-kettle, I have some tea ready for you."

Accepting his invitation with thanks, a tin can of buns was soon in our boat, and never did the lightest tea-buns, served in the daintiest of snowy napkins, taste more delicious. The number we demolished proved our appreciation of his cookery.

About sundown we altered our course. After passing a pretty green hill, from which a group of squaws, children and dogs watched us, we turned to the west and entered Clear Water Bay. The night was getting dark, damp and chilly, the children were sleepy, and were tired and silent. The men on the tug had become tired and drowsy; nothing seemed to stir but the flying sparks from the funnel of the tug, which dropped all around us, and not even a cry from a loon broke through the stillness.

Suddenly—" Here we are ! " rang out from a dozen voices, followed by a heavy splash and a cry of " A man overboard ! " While we peered out into the darkness, dreading we knew not what, a laugh came from the barge. It was only the short stove-pipe, which some one had knocked overboard in the darkness. In our relief at finding that the accident was nothing worse, we quite forgot the future misery of our poor friend the bun-maker, whose cookery would have to be carried on amidst redoubled volumes of smoke. A moment later the light of a camp fire appeared, and leaving the tug the barge was poled up to it. One of the engineers belonging to Mr. C——'s staff came to meet us. He had been ordered into town, and had waited at Clear Water two days for the tug or steamer to take him to the "Angle," intending, if they did not arrive before morning, to cross next day in a canoe.

We were soon comfortably settled in Mr. R——'s tent, while he directed a party of Indians, who seemed to spring up in every direction, to put up another. Some of the men on the barge had tents too; others made great fires, piled with broken branches until the blaze shot up to the tree-tops. The swift, silent movements of the Indians stepping hither and thither, now in the glare of the fire, then lost in the surrounding darkness; the chatter of the men; the barking of the dogs; and the sharp crackle of the blazing logs helped to compose a strange and lively scene. Gradually all grew quiet, and settled down for the night; the Indians, rolling themselves in their blankets, lay down with their feet to the fire; and we felt that this was indeed a fitting ending to our day upon the Lake of the Woods.

I think one always wakes earlier when camping out than when sleeping in a house. Our first night under canvas in the "Nor'-west" was no exception to the rule. We were up and out before five o'clock; yet, early as it was, we found our camping ground almost deserted. The Indians, who were nearly all "packers," employed by the contractors to carry stuff over the portages, had shouldered their packs and gone, and only a few of the men still lingered. One poor fellow had caught several fish, and on being asked what he would take for them, replied that he would gladly exchange a couple for a piece of fat and the loan of a frying-pan to cook his own meal in. This offer was at once accepted, and before long we had some nicely cleaned fish added to our repast. The fire being stirred up, and the kettle set on, I heard groans of despair over the condition of the larder. The tin box which contained all that was left of our supplies, became more difficult to pack the more empty it grew, and being unloaded the night before by hands ignorant of the necessity of keeping it right side up, the salt was spilt into the tea, and the preserves were smeared over all the spoons. There was no bread left, and at last we had to content ourselves with a rather light meal of fish and salted tea, consoled by the reflection that we were near the end of our journey.

The camping-ground did not look at all romantic in the morning. Furniture was scattered everywhere, boxes of all sizes and descriptions were strewn about amidst dead fires and charred branches, and a general air of untidiness and discomfort pervaded everything.

Mr. R—— left us soon after breakfast, and we set out to walk over our first portage.* This led us up a narrow pathway, all hills and hollows; then over a smooth rock with a trail scarcely visible. A nar-

---

* A " portage " is the shore of a cataract, rapid, or chute, along which the Indians carry their canoes and luggage. The Winnipeg River, in its course of 160 miles from the Lake of the Woods to Lake Winnipeg, makes a descent of 360 feet, occasioning falls, rapids, chutes and cataracts, which make its navigation difficult. The portaging, or carrying power of the Indians, says Major Butler, is remarkable ; one man often carrying two hundred-weight for several miles. The skill with which they avoid whirlpools, land below the fall, and re-launch their canoes above it, beyond the power of the current, is unerring, and indispensable to travellers.

row gully succeeded, still wet from the spring rain; then we passed through a belt of low-growing trees leading to a bare rock, its crevices filled with moss white as the rock itself. On reaching the highest point we stopped to rest and look back. Clear Water Bay lay far below us, glistening in the sunlight, and beyond, over the point that forms the bay, the lake and its numberless islands extended for miles. As we descended, we met the packers returning for another load, coming at a light, easy run, one after the other, in Indian file their straps hanging loosely over one arm. Mr. C——'s own man, a handsome, lithe, graceful Indian of the Brant tribe, stepped out of the line to shake hands with us and bid us welcome to the contract, with a natural politeness and grace which would have adorned the drawing-rooms of civilization.

This Indian, rejoicing in the name of Youal Carrière, was tall and slight, lithe as a tiger, and quick as lightning; never at a loss, naturally intelligent, and an adept in almost everything he attempted. Having had a fair commercial education when in Brantford among his own people, he was as good a clerk in an office as guide in the bush or cook in camp. He was a keen politician, and ready to discuss almost any question, yet always respectful and attentive. Although never officious, he managed to make himself indispensable. He was fonder of life in the bush than in town, yet as ready to amuse himself when there as any of his friends; rather inclined to brag of his doings and sayings, and able to tell the best story in camp, whoever might be his comrades.

We soon found ourselves on the shore of a small lake, which obtained its name oddly enough. The first party of surveyors who crossed upset two bags of rice in its waters, and thenceforward it was known as Rice Lake. On reaching the opposite shore, we found a man waiting to cross. He had come down the night before, but all the boats were on the other side.

The second portage was much shorter and more level than the first, and consisted of a pretty woodland track of less than half a mile to Lake Deception, so called from the many times and many ways in which the first surveying party were misled when running the line along its shores. One night, after a hard day's work, they had settled down round their camp fires, and while dozing over their pipes, were roused by a shrill halloo from down the trail. Not having had a mail for weeks, and expecting one hourly, they all turned out to meet the carrier, shouting loudly to guide him to the camp; but they were answered only by the shrill scream of the screech-owl, whose hooting had led them on their bootless chase. Lake Deception is very beautiful, with deep shady bays, high rocky shores, and fair green islands. At the head of one of the bays Mr. C—— had built his house.

As we neared the wharf, where stood a small shanty called by the men "The Fort," with a piece of red cotton doing duty as a flag flying from its roof, a canoe came out to meet us, and a warm welcome from the doctor, an old friend, followed. The Fort contained three rooms, each having a narrow window, and the largest provided with a mud chimney and open fireplace. The furniture comprised a couple of bunk-beds, a few shelves, one table, several stools and benches, washstands built into the corners, and a comfortable sofa, seeming very much out of place, in what, to our eyes, looked anything but a comfortable abode. Yet we were told it was one of the most luxurious shanties on the line.

Our luggage could not be brought over until late in the afternoon, so there was nothing to be done but to exercise our patience and wait, enduring the discomfort of feeling as well as looking as if we had travelled for a week, with all the dust of the Dawson road, as well as all the mud of the muskegs, upon our persons.

CHAPTER X.

Making a New Home—Carrière's Kitchen—The Navvies' *Salle-à-Manger*—A Curious Milking Custom—Insect Plagues—Peterboro' Canoes—Fishing Trips—Mail-day—Indian dread of drowning—The Indian Mail-carrier and his Partner—Talking by Telegraph—A Fire in the Woods.

A DETAILED account of how we spent the few weeks would be of little interest, so I will only give it in outline. We slept in the house and took our meals at the fort, Carrière doing the cooking under a low tent close by, which, as a kitchen, was decidedly a curiosity. It occupied a small space not ten feet square, in only five feet of which we could stand upright, and contained cases of tinned fruits, vegetables, sauces, and meats, barrels of flour and meal, caddies of tea and coffee, a small sheet-iron cooking-stove, all the pots, pans, pasteboards, and all other culinary necessaries. There was also a rickety table, at which the men, often five and six at a time, had their meals, sitting on the nearest case, bag, or barrel. It was so crowded that one wondered how Carrière managed to get up such excellent dinners with such limited accommodation. He also made delicious bread, baking it in a hole in the side of the hill, heated by building a fire round it.

By degrees we moved into the house, as the carpenters moved out, taking their bed of shavings with them; and we found daily amusement in the novelty of our surroundings. The house stood on a slight elevation in the valley above the lake, about a hundred and fifty feet off. To the west was a perpendicular wall of rock, rising to a height of forty or fifty feet, covered with tall pines, moss, and ferns. To the east lay a plot of grass, divided by a deep narrow creek from half a dozen dirty tents occupied by the navvies.

The largest of these had a fire burning before it, over which hung a perpetual kettle of pea-soup. Hard by stood a long table of rough boards, laid on rudely fashioned trestles; another board, narrower, and several inches lower, serving as a seat. This table was set almost as often as the pea-soup was stirred. Its appointments were simple, but satisfactory to the guests. There were tin plates and cups, heavy knives and forks, a pepper pot, a mug of mustard, another of salt, a bottle of pickles, and one of sauce. When dinner was ready, the cook, a little fat man, with an apron tied round his waist, a long red *tuque* on his head, and his shirt-sleeves rolled above his elbows, put his hands to his mouth, and gave a loud halloo. Then from every part of the works poured the men belonging to his mess, going first to the creek to wash their hands. As soon as they were seated, the little fellow filled their plates first with soup and next with pork and beans, out of another steaming pot. Ten minutes of rapid feeding satisfied their appetites, and they adjourned to the fallen trees and scattered logs to enjoy their pipes at leisure.

Vigorously wiping down the table, the cook set it anew for the "officers"—that is, the contractors, engineers, and their assistants; the doctor, paymaster, and any one of similar status, who happened to be *en route* to another part of the line. Their dinner call was a shrill whistle, and their bill of fare differed from the navvies' only in the addition of pies made of dried apples, and an unlimited allowance of pickles and sugar. Their dinner hour, too, was a "movable feast," as in rainy weather they took it between the showers; the navvies did not mind a wetting.

Behind Mr. C——'s house the ground rose more rapidly to the line of railway, and at the north end of the west rock was a fish-pond, which never had any fish in it, although a good deal of attention was paid to stocking it. About four hundred feet to the east is another rock almost as high as the one on the west, beyond which the lake narrows, and the future railway crossing is projected. Of course it took much longer to arrange and make up the necessary useful and ornamental "fixings," as the Yankees call them, for our new house when we were thrown entirely upon our own resources than it would have done in town, where stores and assistants are always to be had; and the saying that "necessity is the mother of invention" was repeatedly verified in our case. Time, therefore, never hung heavily upon our hands, and everything about us having the charm of novelty, gave zest to what to many people would have been but a dull life.

The climate is delightful. A cool fresh breeze always blowing from the lake, tempers the heat, and to a great extent keeps off those foes to comfort in the bush—mosquitoes, black-flies, sand-flies, and deer-flies, or bull-dogs, as they call them there.

Manitoban mosquitoes are larger than those of any other part of Canada, and nothing but smoke will drive them away. Many people who live on the prairies, instead of going for their cattle at milking time, build a smudge (a fire of chips mulched with wet hay or green twigs when well started, to create smoke) near the milk-house, and the cattle will come to the fire to obtain relief from the mosquitoes. The black-flies are smaller, and the first intimation one has of their attack is a small stream of blood trickling down one's neck from behind the ear. They bite and die, but there are myriads to take their place. The black-flies are most troublesome during the day, the mosquitoes at night. Sand-flies, as their name implies, resemble a grain of sand, and their bites are like a thousand red-hot needles piercing the skin at once; they are attracted by a light, and no netting will keep them out. Last, but by no means least, are the deer-flies, great big brutes, larger than the largest blue-bottle fly. They generally devote their attentions to cattle, and I have seen the poor cows rushing madly down the clearing, the bells round their necks jangling wildly, lashing their tails and tossing their heads, never stopping until safe from their tormentors in the shelter of the dark stable. The dogs, too, are often so covered with these wretched pests, that nothing but dragging themselves through the thick underbrush will set them free. Their bite is very venomous. One of the engineers showed me the back of his hand where one had bitten him a few hours before; it was blue and angry-looking, swollen to twice its usual size, and very painful. Fortunately the deer-fly does not bite often.

We were able to explore the lake, as Mr. C—— had two Rice Lake or Peterboro' canoes. These boats are built by a firm in Peterboro', Ontario, and are steadier than birch-bark canoes, though not so light. They are much used in all parts of Canada, although the Indians prefer the birch-bark. We went out almost every evening, named all the bays, points, and islands, caught lots of excellent pike with a trolling line, which relieved the monotony of bacon and ham for breakfast, or went to the net spread at the mouth of a little river or creek emptying into Lake Deception, and brought home great jack-fish weighing from two to six pounds. From a little stream to the north-west of the house we had delicious brook trout, and occasionally large lake trout, from some of the other lakes, presented by the fishermen in their neighbourhood. I weighed one which was over nineteen pounds. Sometimes we took short walks up the line, and through wood-paths made by the men on their way to work. We picked blueberries whenever our hands were not employed in driving off the flies.

But our chief excitement during the week was the arrival of the mail. Our first thought every Thursday morning was, "this is mail-day," and Joe's white canoe was eagerly watched for—often in vain, as storms on the Lake of the Woods, when the canoes could not venture out, delayed its coming until Friday.

Strange as it seems very few Indians can swim, probably from their fear that they shall drown while learning. They believe that, if drowned, their spirits wander for ever in a vain search for the happy hunting-grounds, and no Indian will marry the daughter of one who has met his death in that way, lest the curse should descend to him. Yet they have such faith in their canoes and their own skill in their management of them, that they will go out fearlessly in storms that a white man would never face.

On mail-day our field-glasses were in constant requisition, and whoever was lucky enough to announce the appearance of Joe felt the hero of the hour. There were other canoes as white as Joe's, so after several disappointments I studied the trimming on his hat, and never made a mistake afterwards. Joe was such an important person that I must describe him. He was a short, slight, though broad-shouldered Indian, wearing a grey flannel shirt, striped cloth trousers, alpaca coat, prunella boots, and black felt hat, with several folds of pink and white net twisted round it. He always had a broad grin on his face, and a hearty " Bon jour, nitchee," for every one. The dress of his companion or partner differed from Joe's only in the absence of boots and hat, and wearing the hair braided in two long tails, instead of being cut short.

How we appreciated our letters no one who has not been in the woods, with a mail only once a week, can understand. I remember one day after our mail had arrived, a lad coming in from the shanty to ask if there was anything for him. His sad face, as he turned away on being told that our mail-carrier was no longer allowed to bring mails for the contractors' men, haunted me for days. Poor home-sick boy! he had not heard from his people for months. I often thought of him afterwards, when, the contractor having made arrangements for a mail-carrier independent of the Government, I saw the huge bag brought in every week, and watched the eager crowd of faces waiting for its contents to be distributed.

We had another source of entertainment in the telegraphic communication between Winnipeg and all the houses on the line, one of the staff in the office good-naturedly keeping us posted in current events. Talking to others along the wire always had a strange significance to me, like having an invisible guest talking to us, who could only hear what we chose to repeat. When anything amusing was said, one involuntarily listened for the invisible laughter. This telegraphic conversation was a nuisance in one way, for often in the middle of dinner Mr. C—— would exclaim, "There's D—— calling!" and away he would go, and probably not come back till dinner was cold, the cook cross, and the confusion general.

We were not without visitors, for the doctor, contractors, and engineers were coming and going continually. About the middle of July, 1878, the contractors' head-quarters at Darlington Bay being finished, and more work going on at that end of the line, his officials moved there, and we were left with only a gang of forty men in a shanty near. Our fat cook also went to Bear Lake, about a mile west of the house, which by that time had received the name of Inver Lodge.

One day towards the end of August a rumour reached us that the woods were on fire on the other side of the west hill, and that the flames were travelling towards us. I put on my hat and went up to see if the report were true, and found flames curling along over the moss and underbrush near a sand embankment where two or three men were working. The fire did not look very formidable to me, and on asking the men if there was any danger of its reaching the house, one put down his barrow, and while he slowly wetted the palms of his hands, and rubbed them together, said, "Na fear, me leddie ; a barrowfo' o' sand noo an' then wul keep it fra' gangin' any further." So I went back reassured. But as night came on, the blaze increased so much that it became alarming. Mr. C—— and the men were away at Keewatin, some fifteen miles from us, and could not be back before daylight. A kindly old Irishman, Michael Cahill, who for a drink of butter-milk came in the evenings to work in the garden, offered his services to sit up and watch the fire.

"Not that he thought there was a ha'porth of danger, but, Lord bless them! the misthress and the childre 'ud be frightened." Poor old man! he had a true Irish heart, with an air of better days long vanished, and a deep loyalty to "thim of the ould stock;" and his boasts of grandeur and valiant deeds were mingled with childlike credulity.

The fire was at its height about midnight, and had reached a large tree in a line with our house, when the wind from the lake caught and drove it back. The underbrush soon burned out, but the trees were like pillars of flame, crackling and roaring in the silent night, till they fell with a crash to the ground. Half roused by the noise, old Cahill would mutter something about keeping watch until the master came home. The old fellow had wrapped himself in his great coat, and was sitting on a chair in the yard sound asleep. Fearing that he might catch cold, I woke him, but he treated the insinuation that he had slept a wink with such indignant contempt that I had to leave him to take his chance. The fire burnt itself out before daylight, and we felt as if we had made more fuss than was necessary, when Mr. C—— and the men arrived after four hours' hard paddling. About Ingolf the fires raged so fiercely that the engineers there moved all their valuable instruments and papers into the canoes, and left the shanty to its fate; a change in the wind, however, saved it, driving the flames back when the walls were scorching.

CHAPTER XI.

Irish Wit—Bears?—Death on the Red Pine Lake—A Grave in the Catholic Cemetery—The First Dog-train—A Christmas Fête—Compulsory Temperance—Contraband Goods—The Prisoner wins the Day—Whiskey on the Island—The Smuggler turned Detective—A Fatal Frolic—"Mr. K——'s Legs."

THE chimneys in Mr. C——'s house were built of mud, and one of them, which smoked whenever a fire was lighted, had to be pulled down and rebuilt. The workmen, who were of various nationalities—Carrière an Indian, old Cahill an Irishman, a Scotchman, and a Mennonite, who thumped the mud mortar with a dogged perseverance that was quite amusing—were all engaged on this chimney. One day I heard Carrière contradict an assertion of Cahill's with regard to the work, calling it "a d—d lie!" Stepping back from the foot of the ladder on which Carrière stood, the old Irishman lifted his straw hat with the air of a courtier, and replied politely, "Carrière, ye're a gintleman! an' *that's* another."

Before the chimney was quite finished, Mr. and Mrs. C—— went down to Keewatin to spend a few days, leaving me with the maid and old Cahill to superintend the house-cleaning; and many a half-hour's amusement had I, listening to the old man's reminiscences of Ireland. When he found that I knew and took an interest in many of the people in his country his delight was unbounded. The height of his ambition seemed to be to have "tin min under him," and his greatest trial was "huntin' thim tarmints of cows." He was the butt of all the jokes and tricks in the camps round, yet he took everything good-naturedly; "the boys must have their laugh sometimes" being his only comment. He said he was only thirty-seven, but, according to his own account, he had been "kept at school till he was sixteen, lived tin years on the Knight o' Glynne's estate, and gone fishin' with him in the Shannon, been twenty-five years with Colonel Kitchener in Limerick, siven years undher Mr. Usborne of Arnprior Canady West, and knew the Ottawa as well as any man, two years with his brother in Michigan and two years in Keewatin, and all the fault of the editor of the *Ottawa Times* newspaper, for praisin' up the country and tellin' lies about the wages."

Cahill always dressed in his best on Sunday. How he managed to get up his white shirts was a mystery. To be sure, one was made to last several Sundays, for when one side got dirty he turned the other out. The navvies called him the forest ranger, because he always took the gun with him when he went for the cows, and each day as he passed the shanties on his way back empty-handed, they chaffed him about his want of sport. One evening he returned as usual, apparently empty-handed, but coming into the kitchen for the milk-pails, he produced from his pockets five partridges and four pigeons. When I asked him why he did not carry them to show the men that he did shoot something sometimes, he gave me a knowing look and said, "Shure, I wouldn't give thim that satisfaction."

We were glad of the game, as a change from the continual salt meat and fish, being unable to get fresh meat until November, and then only Montana beef. The second year the contractor bought only Canadian cattle. The difference in the meat is very great, the one being hard and full of thread-like sinews, the other juicy and tender.

One evening in September before the mail went out, I was sitting up late writing letters, when Mrs. C—— in a frightened tone called me to "listen to that queer noise"—a crunching, rustling sound from the rocks west of the house, just as if some heavy animal was making its way through the underbrush and dry moss. Rumours of the vicinity of bears had reached us that day, and we jumped at once to the conclusion that Bruin was upon us. What was to be done? We were quite certain the poor calf, tethered to a stump on the grass plot, would fall an easy victim. Then all the windows were wide open downstairs, and we did not think it probable Bruin would respect the mosquito-netting sufficiently for us to depend upon it as a defence. Mr. C—— and the men were away down the line, and the doctor, who had come in that day, was enjoying a slumber, from which it seemed cruel to disturb him after his hard day's tramp. However, as the noise increased, and seemed nearer every moment, it had to be done. Did you ever try to wake a very sound sleeper, making apparently noise enough to awaken the dead, and when about to give it up in despair have him answer, after your last effort, in a mild, good-naturedly aggravating tone, which impresses you with the belief that he has only closed his eyes for a moment's meditation? Just so did our excellent Esculapius. Imploring him to get up, and telling him that the bears were upon us, I rushed to obey Mrs. C——, who screamed to me to shut all the windows. While I was scrambling on to the kitchen table to reach the last, the doctor appeared, very much *en deshabille*, with his hair rumpled and a general air of incompleteness about him, demanding the whereabouts of the bear; and at the same moment Mrs. C——, in her night-dress, leant over the banisters above, listening with all her ears for the answer. The absurdity of the whole scene so struck me that I could scarcely refrain from laughing outright. Sallying forth, armed with a big stick, the valiant doctor drove out from behind the wood-pile on the rock—a large, half-starved dog, who was trying to worry a meal off the dried hide of a defunct cow!

The night was brilliant; bright moonlight lay like a long string of diamonds on the bosom of the lake; a blue, cloudless sky spread over our heads; but far away to the south a great bank of murky clouds, lined with silver, was momentarily rent by fierce flashes of forked lightning, followed by the muttering of distant thunder.

In November a very sad accident occurred, by which Mr. C—— lost one of his staff. The weather was cold and disagreeable, just the few transition days between the beautiful Indian summer and clear Canadian winter. Until then the thermometer had registered 70° in the shade at noon, but the change had come suddenly, as it always does in Manitoba, and in a few days the smaller lakes had frozen over wholly, but the larger ones only partially. The mail had been delayed in consequence of there being no means of passage either by land or water. On the 10th Mr. W—— and Mr. K—— dined at Inver, and the former resisted all persuasions to remain until the morning, being anxious to reach his station,

Ingolf, next day in time to intercept the expected mail-carrier, and feeling sure he could reach the intermediate station, Kalmar, before dark. He left about three o'clock. What seeming trifles sometimes make all the difference between life and death! That day dinner was half an hour late, an unusual thing in our punctual house; and if he had only had that half-hour more of daylight, his fate would have been changed. He crossed the first three lakes in safety upon the ice, and naturally thought that he should find the fourth equally firm, forgetting that the sun had been shining on the north side with a heat doubled by the high, rocky shore. He attempted to cross, but, alas, never reached the other side.

The next evening (Saturday), not hearing him work the telegraph, Mr. K——, who had been detained at Inver, asked Kalmar when Mr. W—— left, and the answer that he had not seen him told us the sad news at once. Next morning at daybreak a party went in search of the unfortunate man, and found his body not thirty feet from the shore. His hat, profile (or map), and the long pole carried by all who have to cross unsound ice, were floating near. His large boots, which were so strapped round his waist that it was impossible to get them off, had kept him down. The lake (Red Pine) is small but deep, and he had died alone in the forest, with only the giant rocks around him to echo back his dying cries. While I write, memory recalls his laughing air, when telling me that morning how he had tried to cross the narrows of our lake, but had desisted, fearing a ducking on such a cold day; and I, pointing to his immense boots, said they were scarcely fit to wear when running such risks. How little I dreamt what harm they were doomed to do! His great-brown eyes, with the sad, far-away look in them, as if, unknown to himself, they saw into the future; his graceful, manly figure, as he sprang up the hill behind the house, and his cheery "Good-bye, till I see you again" can never be forgotten.

When the winter roads became passable, they took him into Winnipeg, and laid him in the Roman Catholic cemetery there—alone, away from all he loved, without a kindly hand to tend his last resting-place. His death cast a gloom over all our party. Though grieving for him and missing him continually, we could never realize that he was really dead. And the knowledge that it was so even to us made our hearts fill with sympathy for one far away, to whom the sad tidings would have more than the bitterness of death.

Our great excitement after winter had set in in earnest was the arrival of the first dog-train. Hearing the shrill "Marsh-sha" (Marcha) of the driver, we all rushed to the window to see the pretty beasts, in their gaily-worked saddle-cloths and merry bells, come down the hill; then, when a halt was called, to watch them sit down on their haunches and look proudly about them, as if quite aware of the interest they excited. The taboggans they drew were not heavily laden, and as far as I can judge from my limited experience, the dogs are invariably kindly treated by their drivers; all looked well fed and in good condition. During the summer, and sometimes in the winter, when the poor Indians themselves are more than half-starved, it is little wonder that the dogs fare as badly as their masters, and look lean and miserable.

The winter of 1878 was mild and open, more so than had been known in the North-West for thirty years. The snow had vanished almost completely from the portages, and water covered the ice on many of the lakes. When at Christmas, the staff accepted Mrs. C——'s invitation to spend the day at Inver, the question was whether they would come with dogs or canoes? Neither, however, were practicable, and they had to walk—some of them eighteen miles. We amused ourselves icing the cake, inventing devices, with the aid of scraps of telegraph wire, as supports for the upper decorations, decorating the house with cedar and balsam wreaths, and providing as good a dinner as it was possible to obtain in the woods. With the exception of having nothing for our guests to drink, we succeeded tolerably well. Being within the limits of prohibitory laws, it was necessary to ask the Lieutenant-Governor of Manitoba for an especial " permit " to have wine sent out; and we were answered that, " if the men had to do without whisky, the gentlemen might do without wine." So we had to content ourselves with half a glass of sherry each, the remains of some smuggled out with our luggage in the spring.

We soon had proof that the men rebelled against the prohibitory law. The presence of whisky being suspected in a neighbouring camp, a constable who had been but recently appointed, and was anxious to show his zeal, never rested until he had discovered the smuggler and brought him to justice; the clause that the informer was entitled to half the fine of fifty dollars not diminishing his ardour.

To a lawyer the proceedings would have been amusing, for all parties concerned were novices in their respective *rôles*. The justice of the peace, with a great idea of his own importance, the majesty of the law, and the necessity for carrying it out to the the letter, had obtained several manuals for the guidance of county justices of the peace, and stipendiary magistrates, over the technicalities of which he spent many a sleepless hour. No sooner had he mastered the drift of one Act, than the next repealed so many of its clauses that the poor man became hopelessly bewildered. Handcuffs there were none, neither was there a lock-up, and the constable spent his time in keeping guard over the prisoner, being paid two dollars a day for the service. The latter was fed and housed, and, not having been overburdened with work or wages for some time, did not object to the incarceration.

Ultimately he was tried, found guilty, and fined

fifty dollars or a month in jail. Many arguments arose between magistrate and constable, as the latter, having served in the United States, and there learned a smattering of Yankee law, was resolved to make his voice heard in the case. The inability of the prisoner to pay the fine of course made it necessary to fall back upon the alternative—thirty days in jail, which jail was a hundred and odd miles off. There was no conveyance to take him thither; and no roads even if there had been; and the man refused to walk.

"If I had the money I'd pay the fifty and have done with it," he said; "but, not having it, I can't do it. If I am to go to jail, all right—take me; but whoever heard of a man walking there of his own accord?" and he whittled away at the stick in his hand, feeling that he was master of the situation. Being remanded until the next day, to keep up some semblance of proper procedure, he went away quite contentedly, only to return the next day and the next to repeat the same farce. At last both magistrate and constable began to look rather tired, while the prisoner, on the contrary was quite at ease. The wire was down between us and Winnipeg, and no advice could be obtained. So at last the constable, agreeing to forfeit his share of the fine, and the magistrate to take a time-bill on the contractor for the remaining twenty-five dollars, they let the man go, neither of them, I am sure, seeing him depart with regret.

The next whisky seizure that occurred in the neighbourhood was a small two-gallon keg, found in the middle of a barrel of sugar. The load was owned by one man and driven by another, whose consternation at finding he was a holder of contraband goods was so genuine that the authorities thought emptying the whisky on the snow was sufficient punishment—and possibly dreading a repetition of the last trial—let the man go.

Soon afterwards several kegs of whisky were found on an island in the Lake of the Woods. The owner gave himself up, and entered the service of the contractor as especial whisky detective, and such was his vigilance, that no whisky ever passed him. He was quite impartial, not letting even our mail bags go unquestioned, and so was not disliked. During his term the line was quiet and orderly; but, unfortunately, he went into Winnipeg on leave, shot a youth belonging to one of the river steamers in a drunken frolic, and was convicted of the murder.

One day, hearing a very preremptory-sounding knock at the door—a knock at any time being an event—I opened it in haste, to see a short, jaunty-looking man, red-haired, and red-faced, clad in long stockings drawn well over his trousers, and moccasins, a short skin coat tied round his waist with a red sash, and on his head a long red *tuque*.

"Good mornin', miss," said this odd apparition. "I'm come for Mr. K——'s legs." Seeing that I had not the faintest idea of what he meant, he touched his forehead again. "Please, 'm, Mr. K—— sent me for his legs. He said I'd find them in the office;" and the little fellow, who seemed all on springs, craned his neck round to see into the room. Fairly puzzled, I stood aside to let him pass; so in he went, returning instantly with a tripod on his shoulder.

"Here they are, miss," he said cheerfully. "Much obliged. Fine day, miss;" and was off to the lake before I had recovered my surprise at his amazing request and his general absurdity.

CHAPTER XII.

Birds of Passage—An Independent Swede—By Sleigh to Ostersund—A Son of the Forest—Burnt out—A Brave Canadian Girl—Roughing it in the Shanty—The Kitchen-tent—Blasting the Rock—The Perils of Nitro-glycerine—Bitter Jests.

WE had plenty of strange visitors; almost every day men passing along the line came in, either to inquire the distance to the next shanty, or to ask for a meal or a drink of milk. Some showed a friendly disposition, and would entertain us with their full family history. Others, with many professions of gratitude for our kindness, would eat enough to last them a week, one would suppose, and go on their way. Others, more taciturn and independent, took their refreshment in silence, and offered to pay for what they received. One in particular, a tall, slight man, rather advanced in years, came in one morning, and made us understand by signs that he was hungry. When the meal was put before him he sat down, took his hat off—this was something unusual—and upon every offer of more edibles bowed his thanks with much dignity. He could speak neither English nor French, and looked like a Swede. When his repast was finished, he offered by signs to mend shoes as payment. Thinking that he was begging for shoes, we screamed, as every one so oddly does to foreigners—as if it made our language any more intelligible to them—that we had none for him. Seeing we did not understand him, he sat down and went through the pantomime of mending shoes. Still shaking our heads, as we had no shoes to be mended, he, after fumbling in his pockets, produced a quarter, which he pressed us all in turn to take. In vain we tried to make him understand that his breakfast was a gift; going away a step or two, he came back again and again, still offering the quarter. At last, out of all patience, Mr. C—— ordered him off the premises. The stranger went up the hill, but lingered, until the coast was clear, to put the quarter on the ice at the door. Then, thinking perhaps that it might not be seen there by the right people, he stuck it into a crevice between two logs in the shed, and went away whistling merrily, his pride relieved of his obligation, as well as his pocket of his money.

Towards the end of the winter, the sleighing being a little better on the portages, we drove to Ostersund, the nearest house east of us. It was Sunday, the 3rd of March, and a bright, clear, cold day. Our conveyance was a sort of combination arrangement of a long, low platform with one seat, on two bob-sleighs, which platform turned on a pivot independent of the sleighs. This was supposed to be an invention that lessened the bumps and swings experienced by the traveller, who was jolted over the hills and hollows of the rough roads. Rough, indeed, they were—up and down steep hills, among and over huge boulders thrown out by the blasts in adjacent cuttings, along the edge of narrow rocks, where Carriére had to hold on to the sleigh on one side, to keep it from swinging round, and down the face of the jagged cliff, into such deep gullies, that it was a wonder we were not tipped over on the horse's back, or left behind, when he went up the ascent. The problem that chiefly occupied me dur- this wild huntsman-like ride was : If the combination sleigh were indeed a success, what would my sensations have been without it?

On the lakes the road was smooth and delightful, and our old broken-down steed supplied by the Government, derisively dubbed " Pegasus " by Mrs. C——, achieved something approaching a trot. Poor thing! its hide had become so hardened by former cruel treatment, that there was no spot on which the whip had the least effect. We were accompanied by the usual number of dogs, who ran yelping after the rabbits in all directions. On one of the portages we passed an old Indian, clad in a long blue blanket-coat, with a red sash round his waist, and beaded leggings, and moccasins; his long hair was tied back, and a red silk handkerchief was loosely knotted round his brow. He leant upon his old brown gun, and the tall trees, through whose leafless branches the sunshine fell in long streaks on the snow and moss, formed a fitting background for his gaunt figure. Unheeding the hoarse barking of the dogs, he replied to Carrière's " Bon jour " with a guttural

"Bon jour, nitchee;" but until we were out of sight remained in the same attitude.

On the 26th of March, an event happened which startled us all out of the even tenor of our lives. Between ten and eleven in the morning, the roof of our house caught fire from the kitchen chimney, and having no engine or fire extinguisher about the premises, we were houseless, with scarcely anything to call our own, in half an hour. The moment we discovered the fire, we ran to the nearest cutting, where there were twenty men, to ask their assistance. After vainly attempting to get at the fire by chopping away the roof, they could do nothing but save as much property as possible. Mrs. C—— was at Kalmar, and being too excited to remain inactive, I deposited the children in the contractor's shanty, persuading them to stay there until I returned, and went back to the house to save what I could. I had plenty of assistance. Never did men work better. I have seen many a fire in crowded cities, where engines and hundreds of people were at hand, without half the proportionate amount of goods being saved; and what was rescued from the flames was not destroyed by rough handling.

The house was built of logs, the crevices being stuffed with moss, and lined with thick brown paper, the seams of the latter covered with a narrow beading of pine. The roof was lined with tar-paper, which made a dense and blinding smoke. It had been built a year, and was so dry that it burnt like a tinder-box.

The cook, a bright, pretty Canadian girl, in her anxiety to save her kitchen utensils, was caught by the flames, getting her eyebrows and hair singed while making a final dash for the boiler; and in the long weeks that followed before it could be replaced she never ceased to lament her failure. She was worth ten men, and saved many things which we did not think of at the time, but should have found it difficult to do without afterwards.

We were a motley group, sitting and standing on the hill above the creek to watch our house burn to the ground. Navvies of every nation; tall, brawny Scotchmen; jolly-looking Irishmen, their faces a mixture of pity for our misfortune, and enjoyment of the "fun;" stumpy little French Canadians; solemn, stupid-looking Icelanders and Mennonites. Carrière was there on his crutches. Poor fellow! standing knee-deep in the lake to cut ice out had brought on such a severe attack of rheumatism, that it was with difficulty he moved about at all. We were surrounded by a heterogeneous mass of household goods: here a pile of bedding, surmounted by a looking-glass, there a basket of crockery, glass, and china; here a dismantled stove, with the fire yet burning in it, there a clothes-horse, still covered with clean clothes ironed that morning. A heap of wearing apparel, taken out of some cupboard, lay close beside one of the stove-pipes. All round the house were trophies of household furniture, just as they had been carried out—the baby's cradle full of books from the drawing-room table, china vases underneath a heap of dinner plates, and rolls of plans from the office, blown into every corner of the fences. And all the time the house blazed on. Then the fire spread, and ran up the hill at the back, burning the old ice-house and a large tree, which fell to the ground with a crash the moment after the roof fell in. At the same moment a stock of cartridges exploded, and a volley of musketry formed the fitting finale to our fire.

The poor children, who had hitherto been wonderfully good and patient, now became so nervous and frightened that we could scarcely pacify them. Our old friend, the contractor's superintendent, coming back to his shanty shortly after the disaster, with his usual unselfish kindness insisted on giving it up to us, and going himself into a wretched lean-to behind the store, until the house could be rebuilt. It would be difficult to describe the discomfort of the next few days.

Mrs. C—— came home immediately, and we were all busy sorting out the salvage, retaining what was necessary to furnish the shanty, and storing the remainder in a log-house used as a workshop. How we raked amongst the still hot embers in the hope of picking up a relic, or with regretful interest traced the shape of some favourite object in the ashes! As my room was the first burned, I saved nothing but a few clothes, most of which were comparatively useless, silk dresses and a log shanty not being harmonious combinations. All my books, pictures, jewellery, and those odds and ends which, though of little money value, had grown priceless to me from association, were destroyed; and my desk also, containing my notes of dates and places, so that in these pages I have had to trust entirely to memory.

In dry weather the shanty we now occupied was a very tolerable one, built of rough logs, their crevices filled with mud both inside and out; the roof was of logs also, but cut in halves, scooped out, and ingeniously interlaced—thus, ⌒⌒, to allow the water to run off. During the cold weather these logs had been filled with moss, and when the spring rains began the water settled in places, rotted them, and came through.

The shanty was divided into three by a partition reaching half-way to the roof. In the first room stood one bunk-bed filled with straw, in the second were two narrow ones, so close together that two people could not get out of bed at the same time. One small window, half-way between each room, gave light to both. There was no door into the outer room, only a vacant space in the partition. In the centre was an iron stove set in a box of sand. There were two narrow windows on each side, and the only door led into the outer world. When we had made it as comfortable as we could, the outer room had to be telegraph office (the instrument keeping up such a continual ticking that we blessed an odd day when the wire was down) as well as dining-room. The big table filled up half the width of the room, and the sideboard a quarter, leaving the remainder for the sofa, small tables—under which were stored boxes and trunks of various sizes—safe, and chairs. We covered the walls with pictures, nails whereon to hang everything that would hang, and small shelves. The matting saved from the hall covered what was otherwise unoccupied of the shanty floor. In fine weather it was not all unpleasant, as the children and I almost lived out of doors, and even when in the shanty kept our hats on, ready to go out again the moment our office was called on the line; as it was impossible to impress children, aged two and five years respectively, with the fact that their merry chatter and a telegraphic message in course of transition were incompatible.

In wet weather, cooped up as we were, with the roof dripping in a dozen places, their number increasing after every storm; with all our tin pans called into requisition to catch the falling drops, and the children feeling it a duty they owed to society to empty their contents on the floor the moment our backs were turned; with the instrument at work, and the current bad, I was often made desperate by the utter impossibility of keeping the children quiet. Rolling them in a shawl, I would rush out to a tent pitched about ten feet from the shanty door, and used as a kitchen, rather than endure any longer the strain upon my nerves in the shanty. This kitchen-tent had a few rough, heavy planks for floor, and a stove at one end, with the pipe up through the canvas, and the ridge pole and uprights studded with nails, whereon hung cups, jugs, pans, and tins. Two tables stood under the slanting roof, with rows of nails beneath to hold irons and everything else with a handle. There was a small cupboard in one corner, and the others were filled with boxes, barrels, and the maid's trunk. The tent had been used as a cook-house so often that it was perforated by small holes made by flying sparks, and to touch the canvas with one's head was to invoke a shower-bath. Soaking in wet weather and broiling in fine, it was anything but a paradise of cooks, yet it was wonderful how well the maid managed in it, and how neat and tidy she kept it.

We were always intensely interested in the blasting of the cutting about three hundred feet from us. At the sound of the horn we were on the watch to see the men run off behind the rock. Then the smoke curled up, and the report followed, sending the flying stones well into the air, and in a second we could hear them rattle down all round us, on the roof of the shanty and far out into the lake. Hearing the horn one day when quite five hundred feet from the cutting, I turned to watch, believing myself at a safe distance; and as I saw the stones falling, and thought it a heavier charge than usual, I heard the hiss of one fast approaching. Before I could decide whether to run or not it whizzed past —so close to my ear that I could feel the wind it made—and buried itself in the sand not two feet behind me; while another fell within a few inches of my feet in front. Snatching the child who was with me up in my arms, I took care to get some distance further up the hill before the next charge exploded.

One of the engineers told me he had seen stones thrown thirteen hundred feet from a cutting. They use nitro-glycerine, and have had several serious accidents while handling it. One poor lad who was carrying a can weighing fifty pounds up the dump, tripped, and was blown to atoms; part of one foot, stuck in the fork of a tree about a hundred feet off, being all that was found of him. A man lost his sight and one arm from merely striking a rock where some of the horrid stuff had been spilt. Often have I watched the long train of packers coming down the hill, each with a can of glycerine on his back, and wondered how they dared carry it over the rough roads, knowing that one false step would cost them their lives. Once when I was out with the children, the dogs barked furiously at one of these poor men. Calling them off, I seized the opportunity to make some remark about his load. "Ay, miss!" he said, sadly and bitterly; "'tis a main (mean) load fur any man to ha' to carry." Yet, in spite of the danger and the many accidents, I have heard these packers chaffing each other when passing. "It's a warm day," says one. "That's so; but maybe ye'll be warmer 'fore ye're to camp to-night," is the reply. "That's so. D'ye want any word taken to the divil?" Then again, "Where are ye bound for, Jack?" "To h——, I guess." "Take the other train, and keep a berth for me, man!" "Is it ye're coffin ye're carryin', Pat?" ask another. "Faith, ye're right; an' a coroner's inquest into the bargain, Jim!" Yet the wretched expression of these very men proved that they felt the bitterness of death to be in their jests.

CHAPTER XIII.

We lose our Cows—Cahill promoted—Gardening on a New Principle—Onions in Hot-houses—Cahill is hoaxed—Martin the Builder—How the Navvies lived—Sunday in Camp—The Cook's Leap—That "Beautiful Skunk!"—Wild Fruits—Parting.

A FEW weeks after the fire, the C——s had another loss, in the sudden death of two cows. No cause could be assigned for it; unless there might have been poison in the wild hay which they ate, put there by the Indians to kill the foxes. The difficulty of supplying their place on the line in the spring made the loss considerable, especially with children in the house, and no fresh meat attainable.

Carrière had been so completely laid up with rheumatism that he had resigned his post, giving place for our old friend Cahill, who immediately undertook the charge of the garden, which he said he understood thoroughly. Looking one day into the hot-beds, which he seemed to have taken much pride in, I found he had filled more than half the space with different varieties of onions, and another part with carraway seeds! When I asked why he put them in there, he said—

"Shure, ye couldn't have anything betther nor inions. Many's the thousand I've raised in Ireland, when I was with Kurnal Kitchener in Limerick."

After the cress had gone to seed, Mrs. C—— told him to take it out, and sow other things in its place. A little while afterwards, I saw the old fellow transplanting something very carefully, which proved upon investigation to be cress. When I told him it was not worth the trouble, he looked up and said, in a very indignant tone—

"Throw it away, is it? Shure, If I'd known that was all the good it was, it's meself wouldn't have filled me hot-beds wid it! The thrash!"

One day he received a very long, narrow parcel and note through the mail. Early next morning, I saw the old fellow sitting on a stump in the garden, carefully spelling over the letter, which did not seem a long one. When Harry ran up to him, Cahill brought the child back to me, and looking all about to see that no one else was near, said, in a mysterious tone—

"See here, Miss F——. I got a parcel be the mailman yesterday, an' here's the spisification that came wid it. Would you read it, miss, and till me, who you think would send it? I think meself it's a trick, an' I'll be even wid thim yit." And he handed me a crumbled piece of paper about four inches square, on which I read—

"To Michael Cahill, Esq.,
"Office of the Civil Engineer,
"Lake Diception.

"Sir,
"Hearin' ye were lately appointed Governmint gardner, we send a sample of our goods. Eny orders ye can sind will receive prompt attintion.

"Green and Brown, manufacturing company,
"County of Limerick,
"Ireland."

"Of course it's a joke, Cahill," I said. "But where's the sample?"

"Shure, I buried it behind the shanty; it's a

wooden hoe, cut out o' the root of a three. I think I know who sint it," he went on, drawing near, with another cautious look around. It was wrapped up wid some copies of the *Ottawa Citizen* newspaper, an' there are only two min on the line that take it at all. So ye see I can spot them!" Fumbling in his pockets, he produced a scrap of the paper, and, turning it this way and that, discovered some writing which, upon close inspection, proved to be my own name. His tormentors had wrapped it in one of the papers I had lent him.

To describe the old man's wrath and astonishment, mingled with keen sense of fun (for an Irishman *can* see a joke, even against himself), is impossible. I had little trouble in persuading him that to take no notice of either parcel or "spisification" would be the best way to disappoint his foes. Long afterwards, whenever I met him, he gave me a knowing side glance of mutual understanding that was irresistible.

In the mean time, the house was fast being rebuilt on the old site, but on a much improved plan. The former had been a two-story building of squared logs, and, to my eyes, an insult to the landscape.

The new one, a low cottage of rough logs, seemed to fit into the valley without marring the view from any point. The beautiful wooded hill to the north, which had been completely shut out by the old house, now formed a lovely background to the cottage, and garden.

The little Frenchman Martin, the master builder, was another character in his way; a lively, energetic little fellow, whose eyes were everywhere. Not the driving in of a single nail escaped him. Yet, with all his watchfulness, he did more work than any three of his men. The habitual use of salt pork and beans, added to the total absence of vegetable diet during the long winter and summer, had caused scurvy to break out among the men, and poor Martin was suffering very much from it. To keep him in better health until the house was finished, Mrs. C—— supplied him with potatoes, which he ate raw, sliced and soaked in vinegar; and I believe, from a conversation I overheard between him and one of his men, that these raw potatoes, bread, and tea constituted the man's entire food for the last six weeks of his work on the line. Many others had not even the potatoes, yet they daily passed the garden, where lettuces and other vegetables, a cure for their sufferings, grew in profusion, and did not take a leaf. I know, had I been in like position, early training would have gone to the winds, and the Eighth Commandment would have become a dead letter.

We had unusual opportunities of seeing the real life of a navvy while we lived in the shanty. Our men came from nearly all parts of the world—Russia, Sweden, Germany, Holland, Iceland, Ireland, Great Britain, and the Dominion. There were also many Scotch and French half-breeds, as well as full-blooded Indians, among them, the contractors finding that associating the various nationalities in camp was more conducive to peace and obedience than when a large number of fellow-countrymen formed a gang. Next to us, in reality under the same roof, was the store, containing everything a navvy could want—from hats and boots to pickles and tobacco.

Sunday, the only day off work, was the general shopping day, and as it was also mail day, the place was crowded, and the week's news discussed. A little below the store was another large shanty, where about a hundred and twenty men lived, the kitchen ruled over by a tall and rather good-looking Frenchman, who had lived amongst the Indians at Fort Frances so long that he spoke their language as well as they did. "Black Joe," as he was generally called, was an authority amongst the men, and was very fond of a little black poodle, which he cared for as a child, spending all his leisure moments in fondling it and teaching it tricks. He had an assistant named Ironsides, who was not only "cookee," but could sew up and dress a cut as well as the doctor, and his services were very often called into requisition.

Sunday was washing day in camp, too; every tub was in use, and every low branch or rude fence hung with the men's clothes. In one place you would see a man sitting on a stump to have his hair cut; another repairing the week's wear and tear of his garments. A group of interested listeners lie or sit round the happy possessor of the latest paper, who is reading it aloud. Others, of livelier tastes, gather round an accordion-player, who gives the "Marseillaise" with the fire and feeling of a true artist. Some hard workers, whose idea of pleasure is perfect rest, lie on their backs in the sun, with their hats tilted over their faces, sound asleep, heedless of the roars of laughter from a cluster of men, to whom old Cahill is relating one of his most wonderful stories; others stand before a small looking-glass hung against a tree, performing their toilets with immense satisfaction: while more active spirits are on their way to the lake, with their fishing tackle, for a long day's sport.

Card-playing was forbidden in camp. Of course there were a few who gambled in defiance of orders, but when detected they were at once dismissed by the Superintendent, who declared that they ought not to profane the Sabbath. Mr. R—— was strict, and apparently severe with the men, yet he was a general favourite. He avowed one day that he could manage any number of men, but the "weemin were beyond him." The contractor had tried employing women cooks, believing that they would be more economical than the men; but those he engaged were such a trouble to look after, that he declared "either he or thim weemin would have to leave the line." One woman cook was called by the men "7-10," from her great size, and her camp being at 7-10 station. On her way across the Lake of the Woods after her dismissal, the big steamer, as usual, ran on a rock, and the passengers had to be transferred to a row-boat large enough to hold thirty people. "7-10" refusing assistance, and attempting to jump into the boat, jumped completely *over* it, and was dragged out of the water by the laughing crew, who dubbed the rock "7-10's Leap."

Mr. C—— had all the stores of provisions which were saved from the fire put into a small root-house under the north hill. The ice in the lakes having broken up unusually early the bad state of the roads during the winter made it necessary for all supplies brought on the contract to be "packed"—that is, carried on men's backs. Each man being paid two dollars a day, and not averaging more than sixteen miles, made this a very expensive process; consequently our supplies became valuable, only what was absolutely indispensable being sent for till the Dawson road was passable and the steamer running.

L

One morning I saw Cahill peering into the root-house, and evidently watching something with great interest. Then he ran to the shanty for his gun, and my curiosity being aroused, I inquired what was the matter. Touching the brim of his old straw hat, he replied, "Shure, it's fine prey I've got to shoot this mornin', Miss F——. As beautiful a skunk as ever ye see!" and levelling the gun, he was about to shoot, when memories of former odours made me implore him to desist. "But he'll ate all the pork!" the old fellow remonstrated, much aggrieved at being deprived of so fine an opportunity of displaying his prowess. I assured him that, if let alone, the "beautiful skunk" would go quietly away when he had enjoyed a good meal; but, if disturbed, he would use his natural weapon of defence, and destroy everything in the root-house. But—

> "A man convinced against his will
> Is of the same opinion still,"

and old Cahill, though he shouldered his weapon and walked away, grumbled as he went. We paid frequent visits to the root-house that morning to see if the intruder had gone, but he did not leave until the middle of the second day. Skunks, or polecats, are not numerous in that part of the country. The dogs sometimes came in from a hunt very strongly scented by them, but, with the exception of our visitor, we never saw one about the premises. They abound in prairies and swampy grounds, and when attacked the odour they emit is overpowering and indescribable; without exception the worst that ever assailed our nostrils.

As the spring wore on we spent the brightening days in gathering wild-flowers, going fishing, and repeating the weekly routine of a quiet life in the woods. The weather grew hotter, the flies more plentiful, and our highest gratification seemed to be to make a good smudge in the evening, sit round it, and talk. How gladly we welcomed the first strawberries and blueberries which pretty Mrs. Bucketee, as we called her, brought to us! She got the name from always being hungry (*bucketee*) when she came, and she laughed merrily one day when called so inadvertently. We ourselves went out and gathered several pailsful from the rocks on the first portage. Blueberries, or huckleberries as they are called in Ontario, grow much larger in the North-West than I ever saw them elsewhere, being sometimes as large as small Delaware grapes. The little bushes grow thickly in the crevices of the rock, and are so completely covered with fruit that their tiny leaves are scarcely visible. They have a beautiful bloom upon them when fresh, and are cool and delicious to the taste.

Summer swiftly passed and the time drew near when I was to leave Lake Deception, and, after staying a day or two at each of the other houses on the line, turn my steps eastward, back to what my friends called civilized life. It was not without many a heartache that I bade good-bye to the wee bairns whom I loved so dearly, knowing that, though my regrets might be lifelong, in their childish hearts the pain of parting would be but the grief of an hour.

CHAPTER XIV.

For Ostersund—Lake Lulu—Giant Rocks and Pigmy Mortals—The Island Garden — Heaven's Artillery — Strange Casualty at the Ravine—My Luggage nearly blown up—The Driver's Presence of Mind—How to carry a Canoe—Darlington Bay—An Invisible Lake—Lord and Lady Dufferin—A Paddle to the Rapids—The Captain's Tug—Monopoly of Water-carriage — Indian Legends — The Abode of Snakes.

THE 27th of August dawned sultry and oppressive, but having decided to leave Inver for a long-promised visit to Ostersund on that day, and feeling that if I did not get the parting with the children over at once I should never succeed in going away at all, I determined to carry out my intention, although by doing so I was obliged to forego the pleasure of visiting Kalmar, which I regretted very much.

Mr. K—— and Mr. F—— came for me about two o'clock, and sending the man on with my travelling-bag, I prepared to enjoy the first long walk I had taken since I left Ontario. From the top of the east rock I took my last look at the spot where I had spent nearly sixteen months, on which I shall always look back with kindly memories. Clinging to the rough railing, and walking quickly over the floating logs, we were soon across the boom in Lake Deception, and over the first short portage to Lake Beau-Beau—or "Champagne Charlie" Lake—a beautiful sheet of water, with several pretty islands, along whose southern shore the Canada Pacific Railway line runs.

Catching sight of a boat, which probably belonged to a gang of men who were at work with pulleys, removing great fragments of rock from a cutting near, Mr. F—— took possession of it, and we rowed across, ignoring the fatigue of the poor navvies, who after a hard day's work, would have to walk round the lake to recover their property.

On the opposite shore part of the trail lay through a long, narrow valley, where it became such a mere path that two could not walk abreast; then it passed over such lofty hills, and into such sudden dips of valley land, that one could not help speculating as to the immense cost of filling up and levelling to bring the line to a proper grade. We skirted the shores of Lake Lulu, whose blue waters glistened in the afternoon sun, as we caught a momentary glimpse through the trees of a tiny hill, where a clear fresh spring tempted us to sit on the gnarled trunk of a fallen tree and refresh ourselves. How small we felt by involuntary comparison with the gigantic rock towering above our heads, or even with the huge fragments thrown out and scattered at its base! I wonder if future ages will look upon these blocks of stone as we do upon Stonehenge, and conjecture with what powerful weapons we ancients could have moved them from their bed, and thrown them head long into the lovely dell.

I should like to linger over the delightful three weeks I spent at Ostersund, and describe in detail the tranquil pleasures of every day. How we sat working with the children, through long, quiet mornings, on the small space cleared in front of the house, or wandered through the woods in search of mosses and ferns; how we went for long paddles on Lake

Lulu, either in the bright afternoon, when we took the children with us over to the island garden, returning with supplies of ripe red tomatoes, or in the clear, silent evenings, when we pushed out the canoe in any direction—for all were charming—watching the glowing sunset die beyond the hills, and the Indian camp fires wake to life along the shores.

One of the strangest thunderstorms I ever saw raged while I was at Ostersund. The whole day had been warm, and as night fell the air became sultry, and the sky assumed a leaden hue. Directly west of us, the only bit of horizon we could see was across the line of railway; on either side of this, high wooded rocks, some few hundred feet from the line, dropped to a much lower level than that on which the house stood, and beyond the brow of this declivity the sky had the appearance of a huge fire, whose bright-red flames shot up into great clouds of rolling, whirling smoke, their inky hue gradually expanding until the whole sky became covered. Still the flames raged on in a weird stillness broken only by the sound of rushing wind, the crackling and swaying of branches, or a low, distant moan that

warned us the storm was on its way. For more than **half** an hour **we** watched the horizon, scarcely believing that its strange hue was not really the reflection **of** fire in the woods, till, with the **report** as of a thousand cannon crashing **on all sides, and** the fierce blast of a tornado, **the storm was upon us. It spent** itself, however, in that one **blast**; the red light **gradually paled and** died, stars peeped **through the riven clouds,** and the muttering thunder rolled away to **the** south.

A culvert was being built close to the house, and we took the greatest interest in the proceedings of all concerned—from the oxen, with their tinkling bells, labouring up the steep with the **heavy** timbers **in tow,** to the sad-faced contractor **and his jovial,** good-looking partner. **As I stood one** morning watching the latter go up with a springing step to the top, to superintend the placing of a beam, I saw the chain below snap, and at the same instant the huge beam swung round, **striking** the contractor, who, with a groan, fell headlong **to** the bottom of the ravine—a distance of twenty feet. Instantly half a dozen men sprang down and pulled **him** up, while another ran for Mr. K——, who telegraphed for the doctor. Most fortunately a cross stick against which the poor man struck had broken his fall, and except for a few bruises and the shock he was unhurt, and back at work again in a few days.

I lingered on at Ostersund until I heard that my heavy luggage had arrived at Keewatin, *via* Clear Water Bay and the Lake of the Woods, having had a narrow escape on its way over the portage. The horse ran away, and dragged the cart over a number of nitro-glycerine cans. The driver fled in terror, but returned sometime afterward, and was astonished to find an atom of either horse, cart or luggage remaining. The driver was not wanting in bravery either, for a few days before, the left wheel of his cart had come in contact with a stump and turned over, the whole weight of the horse's body falling upon the man. Knowing that the load in the cart was too heavy for the horse to raise unassisted, and that if he struggled he would be pounded to death, he had the presence of mind to seize the brute by the ear, and hold his head to the ground until assistance came—an hour and a half afterwards—when the poor fellow was too exhausted and numbed to get up.

As it was necessary that I should repack my luggage before sending it to Winnipeg, I was obliged to tear myself away from Ostersund, hoping to see my friends again before I left the contract altogether. This hope, however, was not fulfilled, and it was a last farewell I took of them as they stood on the rustic wharf, while Mr. K—— pushed off the birch bark canoe in which I was lounging. Paddling along the east shore, rather close in, as the lake was rough we soon reached the portage to Middle Lake. Lifting the canoe well out of the water, and turning it over, Mr. K—— raised it above his head; then slipping the paddles on his shoulders, and across the bars of the canoe, he carried it with ease up the steep bank and down the hill to the other lake. In this way Indians will carry, or as they call it, "portage," their canoes for long distances. Middle Lake is long, narrow, and swampy-looking, less pretty than any we crossed on our way out. Leaving the canoe at the next portage well drawn in under the trees, and the paddles carefully hidden in the underbrush, lest any stray traveller should take advantage of it, we walked the remaining two miles to Darlington Bay.

The heavy rains of the week before had made parts of the track very wet, but by jumping from one log to another, and utilizing stones scattered from the cuttings, we managed to cross very well. One of the most beautiful spots is where the line crosses War Eagle Rock Lake. Until on the very brow of the rocky, perpendicular shore, one does not suspect the existence of a lake, and when nearly there I laughed as Mr. K—— asked how wide a lake I thought there was between us and the trail leading through some trees apparently close by. A moment later I paused in astonishment. At our feet, full sixty feet below, lying between two walls of rock, which looked as though an earthquake had rent it apart to leave space for the sparkling water, was the lake of the romantic name. Below the boom, which is eighty feet across, the breach widened, leaving space for a tiny rocky island with only sufficient foliage upon it to make it picturesque—a natural fortress to guard the opening into the broad beautiful sheet of water which lay beyond.

A blacksmith's forge hidden amid the trees, with the brawny smith singing over his work, was the only object of interest we passed before reaching Darlington, the contractor's head-quarters, where Mr. K—— was to leave me.

The bay is an arm of the waters of the Winnipeg River, about three miles from its outlet—a low, swampy-looking place. There is a cluster of shanties for the men, and another serving as offices, with a remnant of civilization in one narrow window, in the shape of a doctor's sign; which hangs crooked, however, as if ashamed of the bad company it has got into. Further on are two log-houses with rather more pretension to comfort about them, where the contractor and chief engineer lived. I remained two days with Mrs. W——, the contractor's wife, whose kind hospitality will never be forgotten by me, and went on to Keewatin on Saturday evening. Mr. F——'s house there is built on the top of the high, rocky land which commands a view of the Lake of the Woods and the Winnipeg River, and is close to the portage path over which Lord and Lady Dufferin and their party crossed when on their trip through Manitoba the previous summer, camping at night on the shores of the river.

After spending Sunday morning in packing baggage to be sent by the Dawson route, we went for a paddle up to the rapids. When the canoe had taken us as far as possible, we got out and clambered over the rocks into the foam. The mouth of the Winnipeg is divided into two channels by a large island; the lower, on which we were, is a succession of rapids each more beautiful than the last. Skirting the shore through a pretty, wooded path, we reached a bare hill above the highest rapid. At our feet the water ran smooth and clear round a bend on the river below. A little further it dashed against great rocks, sending the spray whirling in clouds over their heads where jagged edges fretted it as it passed, or forming clear, deep, dark pools between their smooth and solid sides. Then it swirled round a tiny island, beyond which a long ridge of piled-up rocks stretched its bare sides almost across the stream, as though to stay its impetuous course.

The varied expanse of water, framed in overhanging trees, and rocks which rose black against the glowing sky, while the setting sun tinted every jet of spray with crimson and gold, formed a picture I would have liked to carry away with me in more than memory. Over many of the deep pools there were long poles with baited lines, and there, too, the Indians catch large fish with both spear and net.

Half a mile above the rapids we reached the partially bored tunnel through the island which divides the river, the rocks blasted out being used to fill up the embankment at the crossing. A few days before, this spot had been the scene of a narrow escape from drowning. Two gentlemen, who attempted to cross in a birch-bark canoe too near the rapids, were caught by the eddy round the point; the canoe was capsized, and went to pieces over the first rapid, while the canoeists, with great difficulty, swam to the further shore, striking it only a few feet above the rapid—barely enough to save their lives.

Returning from the tunnel, we went into a low-roofed shanty, lately occupied by a family of nine. Its accommodation consisted of bunks built into the wall for beds, with some dirty hay in them, a smoky mud chimney, a hole dug in the middle of the mud floor, to let off the water that dripped through the roof, and the door hanging loose on its dried skin hinges. There was no window, and but for the many gaps between the logs of the walls, the inmates must have had very little air.

On Sunday, the 29th of September, soon after seven o'clock in the morning, loaded with wraps, satchel-bags, and baskets, our travelling party was on the way down a muddy hill to the little tug awaiting it. Our old friend, Captain W——, greeted us enthusiastically, and busied himself in improvising seats for us with our bags and bale of blankets. The little tug had been built by the captain's own hands, and he naturally thought a great deal of it; but in our eyes it seemed the shakiest-looking craft we had ever been afloat in. Blackened with smoke, exposure, and hard usage, it was yet thoroughly seaworthy, and although it rolled about until well under weigh, was not uncomfortable. The stern was roofed, but the rain drove in at the open sides, until we stretched some waterproofs across from one upright to another. The engine fires underneath, where the energetic one-eyed stoker was not sparing of fuel, made it very warm, and before long I found my way round the tiny wheel-house to the bow, and settling myself as comfortably as I could upon a sawhorse, enjoyed my trip over the lake in spite of the drizzling rain.

As we passed the Hudson Bay Company's post at Rat Portage, the man at the wheel pointed out the channel he would take when carrying supplies for the work on the next portion of the Canada Pacific Railway, which would "likely be worked next year;" and the confident tone of monopoly of the traffic on the lake with which the man spoke raised vague speculations as to the mine of wealth this little creaky boat must be to the four men who built and worked it, their expenditure being literally confined to their own provisions, the oil burned in their lanterns, and the cost of cutting the wood for fires.

A long canoe, paddled by two grinning young squaws, shot out from the company's post, and for a time kept alongside us. About nine we entered the Narrows, a passage only just wide enough to allow the tug to pass, and were quickly in the Lake of the Woods. I tried before to recall the impression made by the beauties of this exquisite lake, when crossing it for the first time. Its islands and shores were then clad in all the young verdure of the spring; now they wore all the glory of the autumn, in hues of crimson, yellow, red, and gold—dark pines blending with and forming backgrounds to the loveliest scenes that painter ever traced or pen described. As I sat on the old saw-horse, vainly endeavouring to grasp all the beauty around, the man at the wheel told me the legends of each point and island, gathered from the Ojibbeways during his life among them. If any unwary traveller ran his canoe on yonder great dark island, closely wooded to the shore, braving the wrath of the *Mutaha Manito* (Bad Spirit), who claimed it as his own, storms would be sent over the lake by the offended deity, wrecks and misery alone appeasing him. A Pale-face once, scorning the warning of the Redskin, had landed there, and even dared to build a fire on its shores; but before the sun again set he found an unknown grave in the great lake. Never in the memory of the

Indians had such a terrific storm raged as after the perpetration of the impious act.

Further on we saw, in a broad expanse of water, a long, narrow, lonely island, its trees low and stunted, its underbrush so matted that it would seem impenetrable, where the *Kitchee Manito* (Great Spirit), grieving that the likeness of the *Mutaha Manito*, the *Kennebeck* (serpent), should trouble his children when upon the chase, or in their homes in the good land he had given them, and yet too merciful to destroy, sent his messengers in the silent night to gather all the serpents together. He gave them this island to live in, bidding his children leave them unmolested. And the poor Indian, in his gratitude, has never disobeyed the behest. Another beautiful island is the resting-place of the Great Spirit when he pays his rare visits to earth, and the Indian leaves upon its shores his choicest fish of the first catch of the season, and the first-fruits of the chase as his oblation. Another green hilly island is the grave of the braves, where they are laid until the spirits come to lead them to the happy hunting-grounds.

CHAPTER XV.

Clear Water Bay transformed—Cahill's Farewell—Ptarmigan Bay—A Night under Canvas—"No more Collars or Neckties!"—Companions in Misfortune—Cedar Lake—"Lopsticks"—An Indian Village—Shashegheesh's Two Wives—Buying Potatoes—*Seniores Priores*—Excellent Carrots!—Frank's Flirtations with the Squaws—The Dogs eat Carrière's Toboggan.

TOWARDS noon we turned westward into Clear Water Bay, and were soon at the landing. How changed from the night we landed here nearly a year and a half before! Then it was only a forest traversed by a narrow path; now the scene is crowded with a log storehouse and well-used roads, several shanties, piles of glycerine cans, a barge waiting the arrival of the tug, swarms of boats and canoes, and groups of navvies standing round the storehouse, whence we hear the twang of a rudely played, but not unmusical, violin: Indians and squaws, beside their wigwams, complete the picture.

Here we met our old friend Cahill, who came on board to say good-bye. He had been away haymaking when I left Lake Deception, and I regretted not seeing him. He had made up his mind to leave the country and return to Ontario. In despair because he had not his two trunks with him, so that he could accompany us, he implored us to wait until he went and fetched them, and when we tried to explain that we should have no means of conveying his trunks he drew himself up and informed us with dignity that he could afford to pay his way like any other honest man. But at last, understanding that our mode of travelling would preclude any such weighty baggage as trunks, he bade us farewell and a hearty God-speed, muttering as he walked away that he would not be long after us in "this God-forsaken counthry, that all the gintlefolks were lavin'." I have never heard if he carried out his threat, but wherever he may end his days, I am sure his kind Irish heart will be unchanged.

Taking the barge in tow and our Indians—Carrière, who was to act as guide, and a merry Iroquois named Frank Saddler—coming on board, we steamed out of Clear Water Bay, and in the fast-falling rain reached our landing place, a large rock on a sandy, wooded shore, whence we were to make our first portage into Ptarmigan Bay. The captain let the tug run close up to this rock, and with little difficulty we disembarked on a spot that seemed to lead nowhere. Bidding us a cordial good-bye, good luck, and speedy return all round, the jolly old skipper left us, and we watched the little tug, with the barge hugged close alongside to keep it off the sunken rocks, disappear in the rain.

We decided that it was too wet and late to make any further progress that night, so Carrière and Frank went in search of a camping-ground; and soon the merry ring of their axes, the crash of falling timber, and the crackling of fires, which sent ruddy gleams through the trees, raised our drooping spirits and dried our damp clothes, and no merrier party ever clustered round the welcome blaze. We enjoyed our pan of fried pork and cold roast beef, accompanied by tin pannikins of tea, more thoroughly than the most *recherché* repast served in the most perfectly appointed dining-room. Spreading the waterproofs, sheets and robes on the ground in the tent, Mr. F—— made the bed over its entire width then rolled the ends up, leaving us space to dress. We had a huge fire across the doorway of our tent, and about ten or twelve feet off blazed another fire behind which rose the tent of the gentlemen.

"Now we're in camp, away with the frivolities of civilized life," cried Mr. F——, as he took off his collar and necktie and tossed them into his wife's lap. "I'm not going to put those on again until I get to Winnipeg, and fashion demands the sacrifice; nor coat either—unless," he prudently added, "I'm caught in the rain;" and he looked up at the still weeping clouds.

No ribbons, no bows, no extra adornments, were to be allowed, and next morning, when I appeared with some, I was voted a rebel by the assembled travellers, and in mock politeness offered a stump to sit on, and a knife, fork, and spoon all to myself. Rising at seven, we made our toilets on the shore of the small bay where we had landed the night before, and it required some little practice to wash our faces standing or kneeling on the slippery stones, without getting our skirts wet or letting the water run up our sleeves.

After breakfast we packed up, and the men having taken over the canoes, we all followed, each carrying what we could, through a narrow belt of woods; then the path rounded a grassy swamp to a long, rocky point. Mr. M—— was some distance in front, with the frying-pan in one hand, and a basket containing the knives, forks, etc., in the other, while my load was the lantern, whisky-keg, and a small tin pail of pork. Jush as I reached the rock, Mr. M——, who was feeling his way along the top, and warning me to be careful, slipped, turned, and, vainly trying to grasp the rock, went down on all fours with a run and splash into the lake. Away went Frank after him, shouting with a laugh, "I'll save the frying-pan!"

"What's that?" cried Mrs. F——, who was behind me with a load of shawls.

"Only Mr. M—— in the lake," said I: and adding conceitedly, "Wait a minute, Mr. M——, and I'll come and pull you out"—I stepped upon what was apparently firm ground, and sank to my knees in soft, slimy mud, from which I was with difficulty extricated. When the canoe loads were divided, it was voted unanimously that Mr. M—— and I should be put in the same boat, to sink or swim together.

The day cleared, and we reached our next portage after a three-hours' paddle, from Ptarmigan Bay to a nameless lake, one of the most beautiful I ever saw. The portage is about half a mile long, up a narrow path over a hill, and the men loaded and travelled so well, that in two trips they had carried everything over, while we, though more lightly laden, only accomplished one. Somebody here called attention to the wisdom with which I had chosen my load, as it got lighter at every trip, especially the whisky, which, by the way, was contraband. Of course we gave the lake a name—in fact, it had half a dozen before we left it, one being in honour of the dear little baby, who, through all the discomforts of our trip, enjoyed and bore it best amongst us. But the name it retained was Cedar Lake, from a lovely passage, three or four hundred feet long, between the mainland and an island, each high, rocky bank being covered with large cedars, which almost met overhead. Passing out from among the cedars, Carrière paused a moment; then, steering the canoe in another direction, said—

"This is the way, Mr. M——. I doubted a moment, for I was only over this part of the trail once, nearly four years ago. Four years this Christmas."

"Why, how can you tell which way to take? All the points and islands look alike to me."

"By some landmarks. I paid an Indian a dollar to show me this road, and I never forget. I know the dry wood yonder, and I know the portage by a big stone I cooked my dinner on. There's an old tree fallen in the water by the landing, which will be troublesome," he added. Ten minutes afterwards we reached the spot, and had a great deal of difficulty in getting the said tree out of the way, and ourselves ashore.

This portage is longer than the first, and over quite a steep hill, where, in spite of its diminishing character, I found my load almost more than I could carry, and gladly gave the pork to Frank. It was noon when we reached the mouth of a creek in Shoal Lake. Sitting down comfortably upon a quantity of mown hay on the shore, we had our lunch, the first man over the portage having made a fire, and rested for an hour. The unfortunate Mr. M——, reaching from a log for water, and stumbling in again, afforded us some entertainment, but this time I did not propose to rescue him.

Shoal Lake is about twelve miles long and five wide, and is at times the roughest lake in the chain. Canoes are often wind-bound for days upon its shores, and we congratulated ourselves on our good fortune in having such a fine day to cross in. It was a long twelve miles' paddle. As we crossed the northern end, Carrière pointed out the winter trail to the "Nor'-west Angle," six miles from its southern shores, which could be followed for over nine miles by the lop-sticks in view. The Indians formerly made these lop-sticks only to commemorate some great event, but now they will make one in return for a bag of flour or a feast. Choosing one of the tallest trees, they cut off all the branches, except the very topmost, and their bare stems made them distinguishable from the rest of the forest a long way off.

There is a Hudson Bay Company's post on one of the islands on Shoal Lake, and we could hear the trained dogs there howling dreadfully. About six o'clock we reached Indian Bay, on the northern shore of Shoal Lake. Its entrance is guarded by an island, and round its western point lie the low meadow lands at the mouth of the Falcon River. The Indian village on the shore of the bay comprises but a few scattered log-houses and untidy-looking wigwams of birch bark, most of them empty. The ground about the lodges was planted with potatoes, and upright poles with cross sticks stood near, to dry fish and skins upon. The Indians, with the exception of a few half-grown boys, were all away at the Hudson-Bay trading-post to get their treaty-money, which varied in amount according to their rank in the tribe, the chief getting the immense sum of twenty-five dollars a year. A group of squaws turned out to greet the approach of our canoes, which excited far more interest than ourselves. We went up a long path to the chief's house, where an old squaw with five children, aged from sixteen to three years, lived. Another house close by was inhabited by Shashegheesh's youngest wife, a tall, slight, rather good-looking squaw, wearing a merino skirt and loose cotton jacket. Mr. F——had commissioned Carrière to buy some potatoes of her; but before the bargain was completed, her old rival, a puffy-cheeked, but still handsome woman, came forward, asserting her prior right, assuring us that her potatoes were the best. On this, the younger squaw, without a word of remonstrance, dropped the half-apronful she had gathered; and the old one sending for a birch-bark tray, sold the potatoes off her rival's domains, and pocketed the twenty-five cents. Carrière tried hard to induce her to throw in one or two miserable-looking carrots for the same money; but, laughing derisively, she declined unless he would pay more. Anxious, however, to sell them, she followed us down to the shore, carrots in hand.

We peeped into the house; it was bare of all furniture, a roll of skins and some matting, which they make themselves, being the only things we could see. Yet Shashegheesh is one of the richest chiefs in that part of the country, and has two wives, because he can afford to build and keep two houses. Several other houses, well built and with good mud chimneys, were empty, but, Carrière said, only during the summer.

A tattered birch-bark wigwam near the landing was inhabited by a squaw and half a dozen children. A papoose, laced in his birch-bark cradle, his face covered with blood, was roaring lustily. The squaw said his face was sore, and he had scratched it. His screams increasing at our appearance, she seized hold of the strap the cradle is carried by, and gave it a violent shake, making a queer guttural remark that silenced him at once. The inside of this wigwam was more comfortable than Shashegheesh's house. The floor was strewn with clean cedar-boughs, leaving a round space in the centre, where there were still remains of a fire. The squaw and the girls here, too, were better dressed than the chief's family. One child about ten had a bright pink merino dress, profusely trimmed with narrow black velvet and small white china buttons; her hair was braided with coloured ribbons and beads, strings of beads also encircling her wrists, neck, and ankles. She came out and danced for our entertainment, twisting and whirling about, snapping her fingers over her head, aud tossing her long braids about. Her friends all regarded her performance with evident admiration.

While we looked on, a canoe, laden with cedar-boughs, and paddled by two pretty young squaws, came gliding in along the shore. Frank, who could not understand a word of their language, sat on a log near, and soon peals of merry laughter betrayed a lively flirtation. Close together, the girls sidled up to him; and he, casting insinuating glances at them, poked them in the ribs, when they ran laughing away, hiding behind the low bushes that skirted the shore. Presently they peeped out, to find an expression of utter indifference on Frank's face, as he idly kicked the pebbles at his feet. When they gradually returned to the charge, Frank, with a laughing look at us, said something in his own tongue, to which they listened with finger on lip, looking at each other, as though saying—

"What does it mean? Shall we remain or fly?"

Before they could decide, Frank made a feint to

spring after them, at which they turned, and fled like frightened fawns. Not being followed, they ventured to return, coming closer and closer, until Frank, watching his opportunity, really sprang after them, grasped the prettiest by the elbows, and bent her lithe body back until he could look close into the brown eyes. Then, as she struggled violently, with a laugh he let her free. It was time to embark, and kissing his hand to the girls, he leaped into the canoe and pushed off, we following more slowly, taking a last look of the group on shore—the Indian wigwam, the pretty squaws, leaning sadly against each other as they watched Frank's canoe round the point; the stout matron, still flourishing the emaciated-looking carrots, and shrilly vociferating their perfections to Carrière; and the dancing-girl waving a farewell with a huge cedar bough.

Carrière told us that during the previous winter the village was full, and when he stopped a night there, *en route* from Winnipeg, some of the Indians took his dog-train over to an opposite point for a fiddler who lived there, and all spent the night in a grand "spree" of dancing and drinking. But in the morning only the shattered remains of his toboggan and dogs were to be found, the half-starved native animals having devoured provisions and robes, and gnawed the toboggan to pieces, so that he had to make the best of his way home on foot—a sadder, if not a wiser man.

CHAPTER XVI.

Falcon River—An Unlucky Supper—The Fate of our Fried Pork—A Weary Paddle—A Sundial in the wilderness—A Gipsy Picnic—"Floating away"—The Dried Muskrats—Falcon Lake—How can we land?—Mr. M—— "in again"—Surprised by Indians—How we dried our Clothes—The Last Night in Camp.

HALF an hour after leaving the Indian village we reached Falcon River, a narrow winding stream running in a swamp between hills. About half a mile down we struck our camp for the night, at a spot where a rude wharf or landing of logs had been built by the contractors' haymakers. Inside a rude "corelle," or paddock, where they had kept their cattle, we pitched our tent and made a fire. The night set in so dark and cloudy that, unless within the immediate blaze, it was impossible to see what we were doing. We were hungry, and the added luxury of potatoes made us anxious to have dinner as soon as possible. Carrière brought in wood for the night, Mr. F—— made up our tent, and Mr. M—— superintended the stowage of the canoes, while Frank put our precious potatoes in a tin kettle over the fire, and, in mistaken zeal, the frying-pan of pork at the same time. The latter, of course, was cooked long before the former, so, taking it off the fire, he set it on the ground hard by. Mr. M—— coming up a moment after, and yielding to the universal desire to "poke the fire," stepped into the pan of pork. While we were laughing over his propensity for tumbling into things, Carrière, who, poor fellow, was still suffering terribly from rheumatism, limped up with a log on his shoulder, and also fell foul of the pork. At the same moment a lantern appeared in the distance, carried by Mr. F——, on his return from the canoe. Jumping over the fence, he exclaimed, "By Jove! that blaze is good. I'll get warm before I do anything else," and stepped back splash into the ill-fated pan of pork, making what was left of the contents fly in every direction.

"That's a bad place for it!" said Carrière, coolly picking up the pieces, and putting it on the other side of the fire.

"Are those potatoes boiled yet?" Frank shouted from the darkness, and, being answered in the affirmative, made his appearance with the bag containing our dinner service of tin and other table necessaries. Tea made, drawn, and the potatoes boiled to a turn, Frank prepared to serve up the dinner, but looked in vain for the pork, "I say, Carrière, what have you done with the frying-pan? I left it just here!" he cried, seizing a brand from the fire for a torch. Scarcely had he uttered the words when a stumble and "O Lord!" told us that the pork was really done for this time.

Rain fell heavily all night, but held off in the morning long enough for us to get breakfast and start, which we lost no time in doing as there was a long paddle before us to our next camping-ground. Oh, the windings of that Falcon River! In some parts not more than a canoe's length wide, and in none more than two, it wound in and out, up and down, this way and that. For a hundred feet we were dead against the wind, then a sharp turn sent us spinning along before it, when, standing up, I held the waterproof in my outstretched arms as a sail. Each bend of the shore was so abrupt that the impetus of turning drove the canoe half a length into the long grass, and it was with some difficulty backed out. We were cut off from our companions' canoe, but could see their heads apparently only a few feet from us, as the crow flies; but so numerous were the turns of the river between us, that they were really half a mile behind.

At noon we stopped at another haymakers' deserted camping-ground, and took shelter from the now pouring rain under a lean-to of poles covered with bark. A low shanty near having a rude crank for holding a kettle over the fire, we had a comfortable lunch. Out in the open, where there were remnants of rough cultivation, was a sundial made of a jagged-edged flat piece of tin, the figures scratched with a knife. Carrière said that it was the best camping-ground on the river, and, while a gang of men were there, was very comfortable. Had any one from the more civilized world seen us idly lolling about on the logs or ground in our travelling costumes, the Indians leaning against the uprights, the baby as happy as a queen on an outspread buffalo robe, the tin plates and mugs, knives, forks, and kettles, to say nothing of the whisky-keg, and general *débris* of a finished feast, and at the same time heard the steady, drenching rain descending round us, he might have wondered at the laughter, fun, and chaff in which we all indulged.

But we could not stay there all day, and the rain showing no signs of abating, we set out again. Not far from the camping ground we passed an Indian standing on the bank near two birch-bark canoes, while up on the hill a wretched wigwam sent forth the usual number of squaws, children, and dogs to greet our approach. The Indian had no potatoes, no ducks, no fish, no anything to sell; so, with a "Bon jour, nitchee," we sped on. About this time I noticed that my hat, a brown straw with green leaves somewhere amongst the trimming, was weeping blue tears all down my ulster. Taking the drenched and now almost colourless leaves out, I sent them afloat on the river, mentally resolving that if I ever undertook a journey of the kind again, I would have a casing of waterproof, and leave voluminous skirts and useless adornments at home.

At one of the landing spots was an upright pole, from the top of which hung half a dozen musk-rats, tied together with a red string; and such is the honesty of the Indians, that they might hang there until they rotted off, before any but the rightful owner would touch them.

Carrière said the swamp was full of traps, and pointed out many spots where he knew they were placed to catch the musk-rats, but which to our eyes were undistinguishable from the rest of the swamp.

On, on, down the interminable river. The rain was still falling, and we were all gradually getting numbed and quiet; running into the shore, or spinning before the wind, no longer affording any excitement. We got so far ahead of the other canoe that we could not hear even Mr. F——'s " Whoop it up! " as he called a wild halloo he indulged in whenever he thought our spirits needed raising. Pulling up under the shelter of some bulrushes, for the wind was becoming keener every moment, we waited with chattering teeth until our comrades joined us, when we kept together better for the remainder of the way. During the afternoon we several times crossed the south or first line surveyed for the Canada Pacific, which has been proved by recent inquiries the most inexpensive route. But I could not help pitying the "party" that had to work through such a wretched country.

As we neared the mouth of the river we felt the wind very much, and vague fears of what the weather would be like outside, and what chance there was of landing, began to assail us. However, there was nothing for it but to persevere. When nearly dusk the wash of the waves on the shore warned us that we were on Falcon Lake. Subdued by atmospheric woes, we heard the sound without comment; but it revived the drooping energies of our canoemen, and, putting on a spurt, we were soon across the bay. Beyond the point great white-capped waves tossed and raged before the fury of the wind. If we could only round the point, a good camping-ground awaited us, but it was a question whether the canoes could live through the turn. However, the alternative of landing in a swamp made it worth the attempt. Asking me if I was afraid to venture, and being answered, "Not, if *you* are not!" Mr. M——

headed the canoe towards the lake, and in a moment we were abreast of the point, when Carrière said—

"Better not try it, sir; it is too dark to cross the lake, and on this shore the canoe would be dashed to pieces before we could unload her."

So we turned, and a few vigorous strokes drove the canoe well up into the long grass, where we sat a moment waiting for the next scene of the tragi-comedy. It was Mr. M—— "in again"—but purposely this time. Rolling up their trousers as high as they could, the men jumped into the swamp, and though sinking nearly to their waists, they with a "Heave-ahoy!" pulled the loaded canoe well up to the bank. Then bidding us stay quiet until they got the tents pitched and the fire alight, they left us in the fast-gathering darkness to do that hardest work of all, which generally falls to woman's lot—to wait. As we sat silently there, the baby asleep, the maid telling her woes over the side of the canoe in the most heart-rending manner, we were nearly startled out of our wits by the sudden appearance of a birch-bark canoe propelled by two shaggy-haired Indians, which glided into the swamp alongside of us. Listening to the ring of axes and voices on shore, then pointing to us, they asked some question in their own tongue, which we answered by pointing to the land and nodding. With an " Ugh ! " they left their canoe and went on shore, where they were immediately pressed into the service to unload and gather hay for our beds. They had a " tom-tom "—an instrument something between a drum and a tambourine, which they play at all their feasts and gambling-bouts—a scarlet top-knotted cock of the woods, a small fish, a little birch-bark basket with the lid tightly sewed down, and an old worn-out blanket in their canoe.

It was quite dark by the time we had landed, cramped and cold from our long day on the river. I, however, was the best off, as I had the width of the canoe to myself, and was not afraid to move about a little, while Mrs. F—— had to share her seat with the maid and the baby. We floundered helplessly up the wet path, sinking over our ankles in many places ; but a glorious fire on the top of the height greeted us, and a mug of hot whisky and water—taken medicinally, of course—made us quite ready to eat a hearty dinner and dry our wet clothes. The tent was prepared, and, diving under its folds, we divested ourselves of one garment, and after drying it dived under again, to put it on while we dried the next. Hammering sticks into the ground round the fire, we soon surmounted them with an array of different-sized boots and various-coloured stockings. We held more voluminous articles to the fire ourselves, avoiding the sparks as best we might, and closing our eyes to let the smoke-drawn tears roll slowly down our cheeks, to be opened suddenly by an outcry from the other side of the fire of—

"Look out there, Miss F——; your flannel skirt is burning!"

And as I grasp the precious article, and quench the sparks with my hands, I see through the flames some of his own garments floating into the fire. The wind blows the sticks down, and prostrates an impromptu clothes-line with all its load, while the maid's lugubrious countenance, as she dries petticoat after petticoat and skirt after skirt, set me speculating how much there would be left of her if she took them *all* off. Our Indian visitors sit hugging their knees and holding their bare feet to the fire, gazing at all the trouble we take over our absurd superfluities of clothing with stolid indifference. Frank is lying on the hay near, threatening them with the dire vengeance he will wreak on their backs if they get up in the night and burn the dry wood he has had such difficulty in collecting, and which is to be kept for cooking breakfast; and of how little value their life will be to them if they so much as lay a finger on the tent he is going to leave standing there ready to occupy on his way back. The wilder his threats become, the more expressionless are their faces; not a gleam of intelligence crosses them when he says he knows well enough they can talk English as well as he can.

"Wasn't he taken in once? But never will Redskin impose on him again." And he laughs scornfully at the idea.

We sat up late that night, as the rain had ceased, and we had been so dull all day that we felt bound to make up for it now, especially as this was to be our last night in camp. Frank and Carrière vied with each other in relating their narrow escapes from accidents and scarcity of provisions, when Hudson Bay fare of "one pound of flour, half-a-pound of tea, and one pound of fat pork, or one jack-fish six mile long," would have been appreciated. These stories were varied by anecdotes of people they had travelled with; some trick of speaking or peculiarity of expression or action, cleverly mimicked by the Indians, pointing their story and giving pungency to their wit.

CHAPTER XVII.

Indian Loyalty—A Nap on Falcon Lake—A False Alarm—The Power of Whisky—"Magnificent Water Stretches"—A Striking Contrast—Picnic Lake—How we crossed Hawk Lake—Long Pine Lake—Bachelors' Quarters at Ingolf—We dress for Dinner—Our Last Portage—A Rash Choice—"Grasp your Nettle"—Mr. F——'s Gallantry—Cross Lake—Denmark's Ranche—A Tramp through the Mire.

NEXT morning the sun rose bright and clear; but as there was still a good deal of wind, which was likely to increase as the day advanced, we started early; not, however, before Mr. F—— had sent the strange Indians to shoot some ducks we had heard on the lake. They returned with one old and five young birds, for which they got five cents apiece, and the remnants of our breakfast. We all set to work to pick them at once. Carrière, at my instigation, tried every inducement in his power, offering the Indians three times its value in money, to purchase the little basket of wild rice they had in their canoe, but without success. "It belonged to another Indian, and they had not leave to sell it,". they said, in answer to all his persuasions. We embarked on the Falcon Lake side of the point; the water was still so rough that the canoes had to be held off the rocks to prevent their bumping. Mr. F—— and Frank struck directly across the lake and hugged the western shore; but Mr. M—— and Carrière, trusting to my being a good sailor, kept in the middle of the lake, in a direct course to the portage.

The waves were just high enough to give the canoe a cradle-like motion. Settling myself comfortably, and being covered with a warm rug, I slept soundly until we reached the portage—an hour's paddle—so that I knew very little of the beauties of the lake. Looking back at it as we sat on the shore waiting for the other canoe, its shores seemed hilly, and devoid of bays or foliage. When the others came in, they expressed astonishment that I could sleep when the water was so rough; they could not see us at all times, and feared we were lost, and the reappearance of the canoe, apparently without me in it, had puzzled them not a little. Before we were ready to cross the portage our Indian visitors overtook us and carried some of our baggage. When asked to take a canoe, they looked at it, lifted it, shook their heads, laughed, and told Carrière it was "too heavy; they were not beasts." Mr. F—— offered them a dollar to take it over to the next lake—less than half a mile. "No"—they lifted it again carefully, taking everything out of it—"no; they wouldn't do it for five dollars."

Then Mr. M—— and Frank, putting their folded coats on their shoulders to rest the edge on, took up the canoe, one end on Mr. M——'s left shoulder, and the other on Frank's right, and went off at an easy run, the Indians watching them open-mouthed. Then they again tried the weight of the other, anxious to get the money, but too lazy to earn it. At last Mr. F—— had a "happy thought." Showing the Indians the whisky-keg, and holding the open bunghole to their noses, he made them understand that if they carried the canoe over they should have some of "the cratur" when they returned. This worked like a charm; in two minutes the canoe was hoisted on their shoulders, and they were off at double the pace of the others. Before they returned, Mr. F—— emptied out most of the whisky and replaced it with water, shaking the keg well to give it a flavour. It is against the law to give Indians spirits, but he knew that this mild draught could not hurt them. They were apparently quite satisfied, and left us, promising to bring us some potatoes to the end of the next portage. But either they detected the fraud, and did as Indians generally do when cheated—said nothing at the time, but would rather starve than give one a chance to cheat them again—or they were unable to procure the potatoes ; at all events, we saw no more of them.

The next lake at which we arrived was very picturesque. I asked Carrière its name, but he laughed and replied, "It has no name, Miss F——. It is only one of those 'magnificent water stretches' we hear Mackenzie talking so much about." *

---

* During the debate on the building of the Fort Francis Locks, when justifying their immense cost to the country in order to utilize the water communication, the Honourable Alexander Mackenzie, then leader of the Government, and Minister of Public Works, spoke frequently of the "magnificent water stretches between them and Winnipeg."

We were determined not to allow it to be nameless any longer, and unanimously decided to call it Otley Lake, after the brown-eyed baby. It is a small lake, and soon crossed. A short portage follows, and on the shores of the next and yet smaller lake we stopped for luncheon. The portage was muddy; we had tucked up our skirts as high as we could to keep them out of harm's way, and were standing idly about, watching the maid wash, and Frank cook the ducks, when we heard distant shouting. Before we could decide whence it came, Mr. F——, who had gone out in the canoe to reconnoitre, reappeared; but not alone. Mr. R—— was with him, in a new and spotless suit of Oxford grey, irreproachable collar and cuffs, light-blue neck-tie, and new hat; looking clean, fresh and civilized. What a contrast! Mrs. F——gave her dress a shake, and straightened her hat, while I, in my anxiety to let down the loops in my skirts, made sad havoc amongst the strings; and the maid exclaimed, in a tone of personal injury—

"Law! and we're such figures!"

I reproached him for making us feel our position so keenly. The scene would have made a good caricature: our travel-tossed party, with draggled skirts, and hats shapeless from much drenching rain; the men coatless, collarless, cuffless, with trousers rolled up and hair guiltless of parting; remnants of provisions, dishes, rugs, shawls, and coats littered over the ground,—all in sharp contrast with the perfect type and finished product of civilization landing from the canoe. The very grace with which he lifted his hat as he greeted us made us feel that contrast more!

However, we soon forgave him, we were so glad to see him; especially as he brought the mail-bag. While the men read their letters, I consoled myself for having none with a can of California pears, which were among the many things Mr. R—— brought. Don't misunderstand me, and think I ate them all; but I confess to a fair share. The ducks, too, fried in pork fat, were not bad, and we enjoyed our picnic very much, even though, not having provided for visitors, one did without a fork and another without a spoon, to make them go round. Before leaving the scene of our meeting, the lake was dubbed Picnic Lake. It was only a hundred yards or so across to

Hawk Lake, which looked wild and stormy. But Mr. R—— had crossed in safety a few hours before, so there was really little danger with good men and canoes. It was impossible to remain where we were without provisions, and there was every prospect of the wind's increasing instead of diminishing; so there was nothing for it but to venture.

Our canoe, as usual, took the lead, and shooting beyond an island well into the open, was soon joined by the others. Strict orders were given by our commander-in-chief, Mr. F——, to keep together: Mr. R——and his two men in one canoe to the left towards the middle of the lake, about half a canoe's length ahead, and three away from ours; Mr. F——'s. being about the same distance on the right, and nearest the shore. Thus Mr. R——'s canoe broke the first dash of the wave, and ours made it still less strong against Mr. F——'s. But before long the delight of dancing over the waves made Mr. M—— and Carrière work to such purpose that we regained the lead, Mr. M——shouting, "Here comes another, Carrière! Head her up!" as a great wall of white-capped water rushing down upon us seemed to threaten destruction to our tiny boat; then, with a splash, struck it, dashing the spray over us as we rose above it and were ready for another. As the wave passed behind we could hear it strike the next canoe, and then the wash of the water as it went under. It was great fun, and I could have wished it to last longer, but for a glance at Mrs. F——, who, with white face and compressed lips, clasped her baby closer in her arms, as each wave came. Though of too true metal to make a fuss or give expression to her terror, one could see what she suffered every moment, until, getting to leeward of a large island, the lake became calm and the tension of her nerves relaxed. It took from an hour and a half to two hours to cross Hawk Lake, but to me it seemed only a few minutes.

Turning into a bay to the east, we landed on our last portage before reaching Ingolf. It was a long, wet track, with a narrow ravine in the middle, over which a rude road of loose logs had been made, while down the hills trickled tiny streams and a brawling, moss-bordered brook. There were two trails, and while the Indians and canoe-men took the lower and shorter, we pursued the upper. We were too tired to notice the beauty of the country, and were glad to reach the canoes on Long Pine Lake. We passed parties of men returning from their work, some of whom took charge of our luggage; and all crowding into one canoe, we were soon at Ingolf, the most western station on Contract 15.

Long Pine Lake looked still and pond-like; the weeds and slimy tendrils in the water were too visible, the bank we landed upon was too muddy, and the scattered *débris* of recent building did not add to its attractions. Although the engineers had but lately moved into the house, and one wing of it was still in the workmen's hands, everything was as comfortable and well arranged as good taste could make it. Bachelor's quarters they were—the only house on the contract uninhabited by woman—but the ingenuity and industry with which they had been fitted up more than compensated for her absence.

The walls of the sitting, smoking, and general lounging room were hung with trophies of the chase —Indian work, pictures and photographs of lovely faces from the artist world; while books, papers, and easy chairs tempted one to linger. The dining-room and kitchen were still unfinished. So, when we had shaken ourselves straight, and resumed our despised collars and neckties, Mr. R——took us over in the canoe to the contractor's shanty to dinner. The pretty woman who waited upon us could not complain of the fare not being appreciated. We did full justice to it; lingering until long after dark, telling our adventures and sharpening our wits against each other's. The doctor also joined our party. But a six-o'-clock breakfast and early departure being decided upon, we had to break up at a reasonable hour.

In the morning we found we must keep to the canoe route, instead of going by waggon to Cross Lake as we had intended. Rain had fallen all night, but it was then bright and clear. Long Pine Lake looked better in the sunlight, and the portage to Hawk Lake, to which we had to return in order to reach Cross Lake, unnoticed the night before, was fully enjoyed now. The ground was carpeted ankle-deep with moss of endless variety, and ferns sparkling with rain-drops. Hawk Lake was calm, only a light ripple glittering in the sun where had been white-capped waves before. Crossing the northwest end, we struck a short portage to a tiny lake, across which a few minutes' paddle carried us. It was now comparatively easy work for the men, all the heavy camping baggage having been left at Ingolf, and the remainder, except our hand-satchels, sent on by packers going through to Cross Lake. As Mr. R—— and his men accompanied us, no double trips were necessary.

Our last portage showed many signs of active life; there were several boats left by packers—glycerine cans, large racks on which whitefish-nets were drying, a shanty with a rugged garden round it, besides the well-worn paths which tell of frequent traffic. The men went briskly up the hill with our canoe, and were soon out of sight; but thinking that the lower path was likely to be the coolest and most sheltered, we followed that. It was so pretty and dry for the first half-mile that we congratulated ourselves upon our choice, and pitied the poor men toiling up the rocks in the heat. But our self-satisfaction was short-lived. A few yards further the path began to descend, getting wetter and more swampy at every step. Mr. R——, who carried his paddles, threw them across the mud as bridges, and by taking advantage of all the fallen trees and stumps, we got on pretty well for a time. But the task became more and more difficult every minute. Once, while scrambling along a half-submerged log, I grasped some tall weeds to save myself from falling; they turned out to be stinging nettles, and I do not feel called upon to recommend them as a means of support. Presently Mr. F——, who was in front, called out—

"Hallo! here's a jolly puddle!" and plunged in up to his knees. It was too wide to bridge, the paddles were too narrow to afford us foothold; and before we guessed his intention, Mr. F—— deposited the satchels he carried on the other side, came back and took his wife on his back, saying I was to wait till he returned. The extra weight made him sink deeper in the swamp; and as Mrs. F——'s dress floated on the slimy surface, Mr. R—— followed, and raising it tenderly on the blade of the paddle, the procession moved on; while I, the sole spectator, stood, like a stork, on a stump barely wide enough to support one foot at a time, awaiting my turn.

When we arrived at the lake, a few minutes afterwards, we found the maid, who had gone on with Mr. M—— and the baby, while we were loitering at the last landing, busy removing the mud which encased her clothes. *She* had found no friendly back on which to rise above the swamp, and had accordingly fared badly.

While waiting for the canoes, we spread our shawls on the grassy shore under some trees and sat down. Presently some one regretted the absence of the provision-bag, and the maid regretted that she had not asked how to make the buns we had for breakfast. (She amused us much by her anxiety to collect receipts.) To soothe these mourners, Mr. M——, with some little trouble, produced from one of his pockets a can of salmon.

"Hungry! Oh, yes, we were hungry enough to eat anything." But when the tin was opened, we found that canned salmon, without bread or vinegar, went a long way. Even our hunger could not tempt us to take more than one taste, after which we unanimously resolved not to spoil our appetites for dinner.

Cross Lake is long, narrow, and uninteresting, and the surrounding country flat, though rocky. When we crossed it was quite calm, but Carrière said that it was one of the roughest of the lakes in a storm, the west wind having a clear sweep over it. After paddling for about an hour and a half, when we reached the spot where the railway line crossed a narrow part of the lake, and the embankment was partly filled in, we turned to our left up a narrow, winding creek, very like Falcon River, and in five minutes were at Denmark's Ranche.

Then we climbed up a very muddy bank, and along a still muddier dump, or railroad embankment, to a shanty, a large log-hut with several additions, one of a single room ten feet square. The cook, his wife—a delicate-looking woman—and two children lived here. They welcomed us kindly, and with many apologies for want of space. Their room was neat and clean, and the inmates seemed contented with everything except the mud, which was so deep all round the shanty that it was impossible to go out with any comfort, and the absence of exercise was very much felt. The ranche was always full of people coming and going, so there was no lack of society or news. The room we dined in was large, about twenty feet by sixteen. The table was covered with brown oil-cloth, and had benches along it at one end. The other was filled with temporary bunks like the berths in a steamer, one above the other. The *menu* contained, among other things, a wild goose, roasted and stuffed with a mixture of breadcrumbs and raisins, more like an imitation plum-pudding than anything else, flat pies filled with dried apples, and the inevitable plates of fresh, sliced cheese, which is the chief peculiarity of Ontario farmhouse tables.

While at dinner a heavy shower fell, and we were told that we could form no idea of the state of the road in consequence of so much rain. No vehicle could traverse it, and we must walk the remaining six miles to the end of the track. Mr. M—— went immediately to detain the train until we could reach it; and after saying good-bye to Mr. R——, who returned to Ingolf, we followed, Mr. D—— coming with us to "carry the baby," he said. And so he did, the whole distance; and his own bairns, miles away, had many a hug that day by proxy, I fancy.

Poor Carrière, too, though very lame, rather than let the baggage be left behind, and Mr. K—— inconvenienced, also came. For the first mile it *was* muddy, but, thinking it better than our expectations, we slipped and plodded along very contentedly, stopping every now and then to scrape our boots; but this made our progress slow, and we had no time to waste. Soon the path, or what had once been one, terminated, and we had to jump the drain to the embankment, and climb that. In five minutes our feet weighed pounds, and we understood the navvies' saying, that they "took up land wherever they worked." Goloshes were useless, and we soon discarded them, and, but for fear of hurting my feet with hidden stones or sticks, I would have discarded my shoes too. Still on we plodded, sinking to our ankles at almost every step; it was warm work. At the end of the second mile, near a group of shanties, the road was a little dryer, and a pile of ties gave us a resting-place for a few minutes. After this the road got worse and worse, and trying to walk on the greasy, slippery railway ties scattered about was even more difficult than plodding through the mud. The maid, who entered a protest against the country at every opportunity, was sliding and slipping over these ties in front; glancing down the embankment, three or four feet in depth, she uttered a heartfelt " Thank God! a path at last," and, giving one jump, she sank nearly to her knees in the marsh. The doleful expression of her face, and the hopeless disappointment with which she scrambled up the muddy bank back to the slippery ties, was too much for my gravity. I am afraid my laughter offended the poor girl; and it was scarcely fair, either, as she had borne all the disagreeables far better than people in her class generally do.

CHAPTER XVIII.

Tilford—Pedestrians under Difficulties—The Railway at last—Not exactly a First-class Carriage—The Jules Muskeg—Whitemouth and Broken-Head Rivers—Vagaries of the Engine-driver—The Hotel at St. Boniface—Red River Ferry—Winnipeg—"A Vagabond Heroine"—The Terrier at fault.

WE reached Tilford about six. How we pitied the pretty, sad-looking woman, wife of the engineer, for having to live in a house stranded upon a bank of mud just high enough to keep the water out, and with mud and marsh on all sides for miles, making it impossible to go out! They had no society, and only the bare necessaries of life about them; the mail carrier and the telegraph were their only means of communication with the outside world.

Excusing our travel-stained appearance, they persuaded us to stay to dinner. My hands were so muddy that I tried to keep them under the table as much as possible; but, finding this awkward, I looked to see if it was noticed, and was relieved by finding I had companions in misery.

We left Tilford at seven, and for some little distance the road seemed better. Fortunately, it was a moonlight night, or we should have had difficulty in keeping the trail. For some distance it ran along the muddy dump, then came a great open culvert, with a gang of men sitting round a fire at the bottom. One of them called out as we appeared, "Ye's can't git down here; ye's'll have to go round." Retracing our steps a hundred feet, we found a track down the side to a submerged bridge, which we traversed as quickly as possible, but not without getting wet to our knees in ice-cold water. Next we climbed up a narrow path, so close to the edge that a false step would have precipitated us ten or twelve feet to the rock below. A steep, uneven fragment of path had to be traversed, and we were in the middle of the cutting. Just beyond was another culvert in a more advanced stage; and we walked carefully across a narrow single board, whose ends lay loosely over one another in the careless way in which men generally run up scaffolding, so that one nail is the only thing that keeps them in this world. The planks were slippery, and in the uncertain moonlight we scarcely breathed while crossing them. On, on, through more mud and water, until, about half-past eight, we saw the white-washed walls of the telegraph office at the end of the track, and Mr. M—— came springing down the bank to meet us.

"I have just been asking if you were still at Tilford," he said. "I never thought you could get through but would give in and stay there all night. The engine-driver was getting impatient to be off, so I came to find out."

When we reached the train a load of ties blocked the way, so we had to climb up on a truck, jump down again, and go round a cattle-van to the open truck or freight car, where our luggage was already piled, and on which we were to make our trip to Winnipeg. Spreading the robes on the floor, Mr. M—— piled the bags and valises in the centre for us to lean against, and covered us with blankets and shawls. Before settling down, however, I took

P

friendly advice, and trusting to the covering of the semi-darkness, changed my shoes, throwing the mud-laden ones overboard. Then, when well under the blankets, I was comparatively warm. Carrière and Frank came to say good-bye before the train started. They, poor fellows, had to trudge back to the ranche that night, and I, being perhaps the only one of the party who was never likely to see them again, parted from the kindly, good-natured men with regret. Mr. D—— also left us, with many good wishes and good-byes.

The track was not ballasted for the first forty-five miles, and the car rocked frightfully. The wind was bitterly cold, and we crouched down closer under the blankets, but were unable to keep warm until after ten o'clock, when Mr. F—— stopped the train at Whitemouth and borrowed a roll of blankets from the engineer there. With this additional covering, we succeeded in warming our wet clothes. The dear little baby slept all the time in its mother's arms, as cozy and comfortable as possible. Her only dread was that it might be smothered, and many an anxious peep was taken under its many coverings to make sure of its existence. We talked in snatches; and until after eleven amused ourselves with learning some railway technicalities, in order that we might be able to talk of "when we were out on the line." But as the moonlight faded, we grew very quiet and drowsy. Once, when I was just dropping into a little nap, Mrs. F——'s caution, "Don't go to sleep, or you will roll off!" roused me to the consciousness of not having a sofa or even *terra firma* to repose upon.

On that part of the line the country is flat and uninteresting, entirely muskeg or marsh, with the exception of one small rock cutting, where the necessary drainage formed the principal item in the cost of construction. On each side we could see the long "take off's" glittering in the moonlight, like silver ribbons thrown at random on the grass. The Jules muskeg, about two miles across, was at first only passable when frozen in winter, except for pedestrians, and we heard of several gangs of men who were sent there to work, digging all day and being unable next morning to find any trace of their labours. The only breaks in this monotonous marsh are Whitemouth and Broken-Head Rivers, flowing between wooded shores. The former is about forty miles from Ingolf, and the latter nearly seventy. Both are small streams flowing into the most southerly end of Lake Winnipeg.

At the junction near Selkirk are a small store and bar-room, apparently well patronized, if one may judge from the mental and physical wanderings of a man who asked the way to Winnipeg, and the wild notes of a fiddle issuing from an open doorway. While the train waited for the switch signal, we were too tired to take much note of our surroundings, the appearance of a rail fence between the track and the out-lying country being more suggestive of approaching civilization to our Ontario eyes than anything else.

Receiving the signal, the train backed down the Pembina branch. There the wind was less trying, the road smoother, and we were getting accustomed to our cramped position. Gradually the train slackened, until it almost reached a foot-pace. Scarcely had we begun to wonder what was wrong, when the speed suddenly increased, and after rushing madly along for a few minutes slackened again, without any apparent cause. The man who had held a lantern at the back of our truck from the junction now began to grumble. "What can the driver mean by going at such a rate?" he exclaimed. Then, when the train slackened, he growled, "Hang the fellow, he's gone to sleep!" At last Mr. F—— said he would go into the engine-car and keep the man awake. When we stopped to take in water a few minutes afterwards he left us, and we reached the station at St. Boniface, the terminus of the railway, at three o'clock, without any further anxiety. There were only a couple of sleepy porters at the station, so we left the blankets, etc., lying on the platform until one porter found the man who had the key to the storehouse. Picking up our satchels, and shivering as the cold morning air came in contact with our wet clothes, we went over the prairie a hundred yards or so to a hotel, hastily put up for the accommodation of benighted travellers, there being no means of crossing the Red River for Winnipeg before seven.

The house was crowded to excess, the bar-room was full of noisy revellers, the landlord was in bed, and there were no rooms to be had. We waited at the head of a narrow flight of stairs, while a sleepy porter roused five men from their slumbers in the sitting-room, and heard a grumbling discussion going on behind a half-open door near us, a woman in an injured tone protesting that, "It weren't no good wakin' her! She couldn't help the house not bein' big enough, nor more people coming nor it would hold;" while the man said, "It weren't his'n, neither; but places must be found to put 'um in."

Presently the sitting-room door opened, and a young man, looking as if he had slept in his hat, and used his coat for a pillow, emerged, staring at us as if taking an inventory of our wardrobe, and disappeared downstairs. With a great yawn, and a muttered remark about something being "a d—d shame," a man who looked like a cattle-dealer followed. Then his partner appeared, an energetic, scrubby-looking little man, who informed us that we might enter: which we did, glad to get a place to sit down in; but hastily retreated, on discovering another man just getting up from the floor, and one busy lacing his boots. When the latter raised his head, we recognised our clergyman from the Contract. He had come in over the Dawson route with the poor man who had lost his eyesight and arm by striking the rock where nitro-glycerine had been spilt. His fellow-workmen had among themselves collected eleven hundred dollars towards supporting him, or getting him into some asylum, and he (the clergyman) was now returning by the line.

Mr. M—— went back to the station to fetch a robe and some blankets, which we spread on the floor, and lay down to wait for morning. The room was small—eight by ten feet—the furniture, a short uncomfortable sofa, two chairs, a table, and a couple of pictures, of Pope Leo XII. and St. Joseph. Daylight seemed a long time coming.

Mr. M——looked more like a ghost than anything else. The poor man had walked up and down the station platform all the time. Neither storekeeper nor key being found, he had feared to leave our luggage lying about unguarded.

Crossing the river in the clear bright morning among tidy-looking women going to market, and natty men in clean white shirts and well-brushed clothes, made us feel more disreputable than ever. And we *were* disreputable! Our skirts, draggled and muddy half-way to our waists, clinging and wet still; our hair unbrushed, our faces bespattered with mud, and blackened with smoke and dust from the engine and our night's travel—the railway hotel not having afforded us sufficient water to wash them; while the fatigue and wakeful night gave us a haggard, wobegone, been-out-on-a-spree appearance quite indescribable.

It is a long walk from the Red River ferry to the Canada Pacific Hotel, but our anxiety to arrive there before Winnipeg was abroad, made us get over it as quickly as possible. Haverty, the manager, received us, regretting that until after breakfast he could only let us have one room. Fortunately, I had some friends whom I did not mind disturbing at that early hour, so leaving my satchel to be sent after me, and taking the back streets as much as possible, I went in search of them. The maid who answered my knock was a stranger to me, and, putting on a very forbidding expression of decided refusal, was not, until I told my name, inclined to let me in. My friend was not up, but a few minutes afterwards I was warmly welcomed and given a bath and clean clothes before any one but her husband saw me.

We were detained in Winnipeg nearly a week, waiting for our luggage. Fortunately for me, the friend with whom I took refuge was about my own height, and very kindly lent me what I needed until I could procure garments of my own. This was, however, a great cause of trouble to a little English terrier, of which she made a pet. Recognising her mistress' slippers and dress, she rubbed her head against my feet and was very affectionate, but glancing up at my face and discovering that of a stranger, she jumped back growling. Shortly afterwards, tempted by the familiar clothes, she again made friendly advances, only to snarl out her disapproval upon hearing my voice; evidently feeling so puzzled and imposed upon, that, until I had my own clothes, she declined to make friends with me at all. Every one was so kind that the days in Winnipeg were all too short; but the luggage arriving on Wednesday, October the 10th, left us no further excuse to remain, and with many regrets at parting, I said good-bye.

CHAPTER XIX.

The *Minnesota* again—Souvenirs of Lord and Lady Dufferin—From Winnipeg by Red River—*Compagnons de Voyage*—A Model Farm—" Bees "—Manitoba a good Field for Emigrants—Changes at Fisher's Landing—A Mild Excitement for Sundays—Racing with Prairie Fires—Glyndon—Humours of a Pullman Sleeping Car—Lichfield.

WE came up the Red River in the *Minnesota*, the vessel in which I had gone down two years and a half before; the same, too, used by Lord and Lady Dufferin, with their party. Some Americans who were with us good-temperedly vied with each other in their efforts to get the state-rooms occupied by the vice-regal party, and the steward was asked many questions as to their sayings and doings. All the Americans took great interest in everything about them; carrying their admiration to the extent of making birch-bark-covered needle-books of the coarse red flannel spread upon the ground for Lord

Dufferin to walk upon—intending them as valuable souvenirs for their friends.

We left Winnipeg about noon, for three days' monotonous trip on the river. Novel or work in hand, we went into the saloon to read or work, furtively study our fellow-travellers, and by-and-by make acquaintance with them. We were a motley group. Round one table gathered a knot of chatty Americans, evidently travelling together, and quite as much at home on board the boat as in their own drawing-room. Besides this party of friends, there were plenty of solitary units, of more or less amusing characteristics: a pretty, merry woman of about thirty, mother of three children; a handsome old lady, hard at work on an embroidered table-cloth—a present, she told us, for a friend, to whose wedding she was going; a young clergyman, whose walk, expression, and general appearance betrayed his ritualistic tendencies, and who strolled up and down, now and then stopping to join in the ladies' conversation. A sad-looking woman lay on the sofa, trying to hide her tear-stained face behind a newspaper which was never turned, the columns to her containing only regrets for dear friends left behind. A fussy old lady in a fashionable cap and cannon curls, after informing us that she was Mrs. B——, of ——, drew her chair near every *tête-à tête* couple, and, politely requesting to be allowed to take part in the conversation, gradually usurped it all, till, before she had apparently quite satisfied herself upon every one's private affairs, she was left at liberty to join another group. A tall, delicate, sad-looking man, the defeated candidate for ——, was returning to Ontario, where he was soon after elected for another constituency. A sleepy-looking young Frenchman and his more lively friend, an energetic speculator, who had gone to Manitoba prospecting for land, were returning disgusted, having seen, "dem' it, nothing but mud." A poor old lady was kept in subjection by a tall daughter, with a face so closely veiled that our curiosity was aroused. Not until the third day did I come upon her—suddenly—while her face was uncovered, and then no longer wondered that she tried to conceal the dreadful squint nature had given her. There were, also, a would-be-fast-if-she-could young lady of eighteen, who had apparently read in novels of flirtations on board steamers, until she hoped to make the same experiences her own, and had not woman's wit enough to hide her disappointment; and a nice-looking girl going home to get her wedding garments ready, who moaned over the long journey to be taken again in six weeks, hoping to be asked "why the necessity?" Finally a professor and his pretty, lady-like wife, and one or two other nice people, made up our *compagnons de voyage*.

I have already mentioned Red River and its many windings, which it is needless to allude to here. We passed Grand Forks at midnight on Saturday, and, leaving an order for stages to be sent on in the morning to overtake us, got off the steamer at ten o'clock on Sunday, saving more than a day on the river by driving to Fisher's Landing. The farm, where we went ashore, is owned by an Ontario emigrant. The house is situated in the midst of a beautiful grove of oak and birch, among which grassy avenues, with huge branches meeting overhead, formed roads to the neat farmyards and granaries. A big bell hung on cross poles at the entrance to one of the avenues leading to what was once the rolling prairie, now fields of grain—six hundred acres, without a fence, stump, or ditch to mar the effect. The clear line of the horizon was broken only by another farmhouse, owned by a brother-in-law, whose farm lay beyond. The man told us he had emigrated six years before to Manitoba, and had gone as far as Emerson, where the mud frightened him; and, turning back, he had taken up this land, paying a dollar and a quarter an acre for it, and had succeeded so well, that at the end of the second year it had paid all expenses. Since then he had built a good house and barns, and bought extra stock, and he was putting money in the bank. The only trouble he had was the difficulty of getting men at harvest time, the farms being too scattered to be able to follow the Ontario plan of "Bees;" * and he often had to work eighteen

---

* "Bees" are gatherings from all the neighbouring farm-

or twenty hours running, the late and early daylight, as well as the bright, clear moonlight, helping him.

The Yankee emigration agents have a powerful assistant in the Pembina mud, in persuading Canadian emigrants to remain in Dakota or Minnesota. But if these emigrants were less impatient or less easily persuaded, they would find quite as good, if not better land, in Manitoba than on the American side of the line, besides being under our Queen and laws.

The stage was so long in coming, that some of our party took advantage of the farmer's offer to drive them to Fisher's Landing for seventy-five cents a head. We were not long in following them, and

---

houses to assist at any special work, such as a " threshing bee," a " raising" or " building bee." When ready to build, the farmer apprises all his neighbours of the date fixed, and they come to his assistance with all their teams and men, expecting the same help from him when they require it. They have " bees " for everything, the men for outdoor work, and the women for indoor ; such as quilting or paring apples for drying, when they often pare, cut, and string several barrels in one afternoon. When the young men join them, they finish the evening with high tea, games, and a dance.

after jolting for an hour and a half over a rough road, most of it through farms, we reached Fisher's. How changed the place was since we stopped there on our way up! We found a uniform row of painted wooden houses, shops, offices, ware-rooms, and boarding houses, besides several saloons and billiard-rooms. Up the slight hill to the south, where had been rude board shanties, mud and chaos, one or two pretty cottages had been built, having green blinds, and neatly arranged gardens and lawns. A medium-sized wharf and gravelled banks had arisen where was only a dismal swamp, while away over the prairie lay the iron rails of the St. Vincent and St. Paul extension line, soon to be running in connection with the Pembina branch of the Canada Pacific at the boundary, when the tedious trip upon Red River can be avoided. The side tracks were full of loaded freight, and cars waiting to tranship at the wharf, the steamer which left Winnipeg two days before we did having only just arrived.

In spite of the external improvement in the Landing, it had not improved in morals, and is quoted in all the country round as the refuge of all the thieves, gamblers, drunkards, and cut-throats from both Canada and the United States. Certainly the men we saw lounging about looked anything but prepossessing. Hearing some shots fired during the afternoon, I was told with a shrug—

"There's some one got a bullet in him! There's always something of that sort happening on Sunday. They can't work, so need some excitement. It does not matter much, as there is no law in the place, and they manage to bring their scores out pretty even in the end, without any fuss about it."

Probably, however, the town is not quite so black as it is painted, and though not a desirable place of residence, it might be worse.

All the afternoon we heard at intervals the whistle of the boat we had left—so near that we began to regret the two dollars' additional expense of the stage. But we were told that, although scarcely a mile off as the crow flies, it was, such are the windings of the river, at least twelve or fourteen hours' journey from the Landing. We left at a little after four, and until dark, when rain fell, we raced with numbers of prairie fires; some great walls of smoke and flame, others mere narrow strips of fire, all travelling in straight lines, and not interfering with each other. A tiny spark from the engine would ignite a fresh spot, and before our car had passed it had begun its race with the others. The driver, who was a new hand, and ignorant of the road, dashed over it at a breakneck pace, the cars swaying from side to side like a ship in a storm. At Glyndon we took on a Pullman sleeping car, when there was a scramble for berths; a section containing two, an upper and lower, costing four dollars for one night. Mrs. F—— and the baby taking the lower one, I prepared to climb into the upper. Divesting myself of my hat, dress, and boots in the dressing-room at the end of the car, I put on an ulster, and mounting the steps, held by the shining darkey attendant, went aloft. The space between the bed and the roof was so small that it was impossible to sit upright; but the difficulties of getting comfortable were compensated for by the amusement afforded me by my neighbours, separated only by a thin slide, or the heavy curtains hung on poles in front.

From one side came the expostulations of an elderly man with a young Frenchman upon his demand for a berth, it being more proper that ladies should be provided for first; all his eloquence being answered only by a fretful, " But I wants my sleep; I have vera much fatigue!" On the other side a choleric old man growled anathemas at his boots and the absence of a boot-jack, which gradually changed into fierce snorts and rumblings as of approaching earthquakes, terminating in startling explosions.

Opposite me, some one, after turning and twisting about for a while, at last thrust a dishevelled head between the curtains, and in shrill accents requested the porter to open the ventilator—"she was just melting!" Scarcely was her request complied with, than a night-capped, grizzled head appeared from the other side, and in stentorian tones demanded, where the deuce the wind was coming from? "Shut that confounded thing, or I'll break your bones;" to which, however, the porter paid no heed, and the grizzled head grumbled itself to sleep again, muttering threats of reporting him in the morning.

It was very hot, and I found it impossible to sleep. The strangeness of my surroundings, and the occasional thinking aloud of my neighbours, kept me wakeful. We stopped at seven, at Lichfield, to breakfast, where, for the moderate charge of seventy-five cents each, a cup of bad coffee, a roll, and some fat bacon were served.

CHAPTER XX.

Lakes Smith and Howard—Lovely Lake Scenery—Long Lake—The Little American—" Wait till you see our Minnetaunka!"—Minneanopolis—Villa Hotels—A Holiday Town—The Great Flour Mills—St. Paul's—Our American Cousins—The French Canadian's Story—Kind-hearted Fellow-passengers—A New Way of Travelling together—The Mississippi—Milwaukee, the Prettiest Town in Wisconsin—School-houses—A Peep at Chicago—Market Prices—Pigs!—The Fairy Tales of Progress—Scotch Incredulity—Detroit Ferry—Hamilton—Good-by to my Readers.

ON leaving Lichfield our road lay through some beautiful, slightly undulating country. Between lofty bluffs, the train emerged along the shores of a lovely lake, and before its beauties had disappeared, another and another followed in rapid succession. The first two, Smith and Howard, are very much alike. Then we passed through two o three pretty little villages, their streets avenues of trees, the roads as well kept as the drive of an English park, the houses and gardens marvels of neatness, and glorious with flowers, and the orchards laden with ripe fruit. As we passed Long Lake, a narrow sheet of water that called forth expressions of admiration from us all, a bright little American child, with whom we had made friends, said shyly—

"You think that pretty. Wait till you see our lake—our Minnetaunka : they call it Wayzata now !" she added sadly.

We did see it by noon, and its beauties justified the preference. Minnetaunka—let us keep the old name which the child seemed to love so well—about twenty-five miles long, is full of islands kept in perfect order. Their natural beauties are developed with the taste and skill that characterize the American nation, by the inhabitants of the beautiful villas scattered along its shores. Tiny yachts and skiffs lay at anchor, or, with all sails set, skimmed the glistening water, bearing no doubt, pleasure parties from the pretty villa hotels, which could only be distinguished from private houses by the numerous chairs and newspaper-readers on their verandahs. A little steam-yacht lay at the wharf, while a merry party of young people, laden with picnic baskets, embarked. When the train sped on, and we had strained our eyes for the last peep, the child, watching our faces, asked—

"It *is* beautiful, isn't it?"

We had no words to tell her how lovely we thought it. Cedar Lake, which we passed before reaching Minneanopolis, could not bear the comparison. An old man, pointing out some large flour-mills near the road, told us of a terrible explosion there in 1877, when many lives were lost. The machinery and mills were shattered to pieces, and thousands of pounds' worth of damage was done; yet in 1878 they were again in full working order, and as celebrated as ever for the fineness of their flour.

At St. Paul's we changed trains, and said good-bye to the charming Americans who had been the pleasantest of travelling companions.

On the Chicago and Milwaukee line which we now took, we saw more of the American element, and felt Uncle Sam's land a greater reality. Every man was a colonel or general; every woman was neat and pretty, but painfully slight. All were perfectly at home; no matter how long the journey, they did not get so tossed and travel-stained as we Canadians.

Before the train left St. Paul's we heard the story of a poor little French Canadian woman. She was returning to Quebec from Fort McLeod, eleven hundred miles from Winnipeg, in the North-West territories. She had gone there to settle, but a terrible home-sickness for her own people had impelled her to spend nearly her last shilling in the payment of her passage back. Now she came in great distress to tell of the loss of her pocket-book, containing her tickets, and all she had to buy food and lodging on the way. A generous compatriot said he would see that she was provided for; and the railway officials offering to give her a through ticket for less than half price, the money was soon collected from amongst the passengers, the Yankees being the most liberal. The poor thing, drying her eyes, acknowledged her gratitude with all the expressive gesticulation of her race.

Comedy and tragedy jostle each other in life. At St. Paul's, also, our sleepy Frenchman and a friend, who had left Winnipeg together to be travelling companions to Ottawa, discovered that their tickets were for different routes, and they had to separate. They met again at Chicago, only to say good-bye once more, their routes still not agreeing. At Toronto they again encountered, to separate at Brockville. One went by the "Canada Central," and the other the "St. Lawrence and Ottawa" at Prescott; so each entered Ottawa at opposite ends. And, as one of them said, "The best of the fun is, my baggage goes with T——, and I travel *sans* everythink."

From St. Paul's our road lay along the banks of the most beautiful part of the Mississippi river, which, shallow though it is, is also broad, bright and clear. The surrounding country was in the height of its summer beauty. Charming villages nestled under the high banks ; houses were built on projecting shelves of rock, with so little space between them, that it seemed as if a slight shove would precipitate them over the edge. Every foot of ground was utilized, and there was none of the *débris* that hangs about the back yards and odd corners of Canadian villages. At every wharf were numbers of small craft and river steamers, seemingly plying a thriving trade.

We passed Milwaukee—the prettiest town in the State of Wisconsin—at night, and could only see, through the misty darkness, its many light and tidy streets. A noticeable feature in all the villages, however small, was the size of the substantial buildings devoted to education. Many of them were very handsome, with grounds prettily laid out and well kept, while the surrounding hamlets are merely groups of neat little wooden cottages.

We had only an hour in Chicago, and saw no more of the Western metropolis than could be gleaned in a drive through to the station, or Great Western depôt. Here the remainder of our Winnipeg friends left us. Anxious to telegraph to friends in Toronto, I, with some questioning, found my way through a large baggage office, crowded with packages and porters, up a rickety outside staircase to a small room in a blackened row of buildings. My telegrams despatched, I wandered through some of the neighbouring streets in search of a restaurant, whereat to replenish our luncheon-basket. Out of mere curiosity I asked the price of the different edibles displayed on the counter. A cold roast fowl, weighing, possibly, a fraction over a pound, was seventy cents; delicious fresh rolls, twelve cents a dozen; buttermilk on draught, six cents a glass; English ale, fifty cents a pint bottle; black pudding, two cents a pound; and as much cold roast pork and beans, or boiled ham, as I liked for seventy cents. The man smiled at my ignorance in asking the price of pork in Chicago—the great pork-packing centre of the West.

As our train left, we passed car-loads of fat hogs, lying two or three deep, waiting to be unloaded at some one or other of the great establishments, where, in but a few minutes, the pig is killed, dressed, cut up and packed ready for shipment again as pork. The public gardens in the suburbs, surrounded with handsome private residences, are pretty, but until we reached Detroit, there was little to interest us in the country. Inside we had the usual mixture of travelling companions. An animated discussion arose between two old farmers, one returning to Ontario from a short visit to a son in California, the other going to Canada after an absence of over thirty years. The former called forth the latter's expressions of wonder by recounting all the changes and improvements he would find. More and more incredible they sounded. A city where he had left a swamp; thriving farms and villages where he remembered dense woods, traversed alone by wolves and bears; mills in the midst of impassable rapids; bridges over falls no man dare cross in his day; and when at last he was told that, instead of getting out and entering boats at Detroit, the train, engine, and all ran on board the iron ferry boat, and was taken across intact, then carrying us through to Hamilton, he bustled out of his seat in great indignation, exclaiming—

"Hoot, mon, I'll na believe ony mair o' yure lies; I'm na sic an ould fule as ye tak' me for. The hale train on a boat, indeed!" and he indignantly placed himself at the other end of the car, his informant only rubbing his hands together in great glee at the fun.

The little black porter on the Pullman was very attentive, getting coffee for us at the different stations, seeing our baggage through the custom-house at Detroit, and when the train was on the boat, and it was fairly under weigh, taking me down into the engine-rooms, where I could look and wonder at the power propelling the boat, laden with two trains across the river. On deck, the lights from the numerous ships and buildings enabled me to see an outline of the city and river; but I wished it had been daylight or even moonlight, for then I could have seen everything to greater advantage. Returning to the car, I passed the incredulous Scotchman standing open-mouthed near the machinery, and watched him as he walked to the gangway muttering, "Ay, it is a boat, after a'. Weel, weel, wonders wull never cease." On Canadian soil again, and speeding on to the end of our journey, we stopped nowhere until we reached Hamilton, at three o'clock in the morning of Wednesday, October 16th. There my brother met us, and after spending the remainder of the night, or rather morning, at the Royal Hotel, we went on to Toronto by the nine o'clock train, reaching that place before noon. There, too, I will leave my readers, asking their indulgence for this simple account of my trip to and life in Manitoba.

THE END.

www.ingramcontent.com/pod-product-compliance
Lightning Source LLC
Chambersburg PA
CBHW031954230426
43672CB00010B/2152